The Blue Ghost

The Ship That Couldn't Be Sunk

By Art Giberson

The Blue Ghost

The Ship That Couldn't Be Sunk

by

Art Giberson

Revised Third Edition
© Copyright 2015, Art Giberson

ISBN 13: 978-1-891118-67-8
ISBN 10: 1-891118-67-6

Published by
Wind Canyon Books
P.O. Box 7035
Stockton, California 95267
1-702-503-7474
books@windcanyonbooks.com
www.windcanyonbooks.com

Cover Design: Wind Canyon Books ©2015

Printed and manufactured in the United States of America by MK Printing, Inc., Santa Ana, California

Dedication

To everyone who served aboard the *U.S.S. Lexington* (CV-16, AVT-16) from 1943 to 1991, and to the staff and volunteers of the *U.S.S. Lexington* Museum On The Bay:

Well Done

Contents

About the Author

Art Giberson

Art Giberson is a graduate of the New York Institute of Photography, Syracuse University (Navy Photojournalism Program), the Naval Schools of Photography and the Navy Motion Picture School. He retired from the Navy in May 1977 as a Chief Photographer's Mate after 22 years of active service. He was the Managing Editor of *Gosport,* a Navy weekly newspaper which has been the recipient of numerous awards for journalistic excellence.

In addition to *The Blue Ghost,* Giberson is the author of *Wall South,* a pictorial history of the Vietnam Veterans Memorial in Pensacola, Florida, *Eyes of the Fleet*, a history of Naval photography, and *Photojournalist,* an adventure novel about a Navy combat photojournalist.

An active freelance writer and award-winning journalist, Giberson is a frequent contributor to various national periodicals. He is an active member of the Society of Professional Journalists, the National Press Photographers Association, the National Association of Naval Photography, the International Combat Camera Association, the Vietnam Veterans of Northwest Florida, the Wall South Foundation, the Veterans of Foreign Wars (Post 706) and has twice served as president of the Pensacola Press Club.

Foreword

This book begins with the renaming of the *USS Cabot* to *USS Lexington*—the fifth of her name—in June 1942. It moves on to chronicle the various designations of the ship also known as *The Blue Ghost* and *Lady Lex*—these designations being that of Fleet Aircraft Carrier (CV), Attack Carrier (CVA), Antisubmarine Carrier (CVS), Training Carrier (CVT), and Auxiliary Training Carrier (AVT). The book concludes with the decommissioning of the *Lexington* and her subsequent move to Corpus Christi in January 1992, thus documenting nearly 50 years of service and duty. This is not the end of the history of the *Lexington* however, as over the next 21 years she has taken on a second life as the *USS Lexington* Museum on the Bay, a world-class aircraft carrier museum—a CVM if you please.

After Pensacola declined a bid by the *Lexington* Museum Foundation to acquire the historic carrier as a memorial and museum, Corpus Christi's formal application to the Navy to obtain *Lexington* as a museum ship won out over Quincy, Massachusetts, where she was built, and Mobile, Alabama. The Corpus Christi Area Economic Development Commission brought together prominent community leaders (dubbed Landing Force 16) to form a fund-raising campaign which, along with a Corpus Christi City bond issue of $3 million, allowed the preparation of a successful proposal to Secretary of the Navy Lawrence Garrett, III.

After spending her first five months in Texas at the Navy base at Ingleside, *Lexington* was towed to North Beach and her final berth. She had been officially signed over to city officials by the United States Navy on 17 June 1992. After a soft opening in October, the museum was formally dedicated on 14 November—witnessed by former crew members, and members of numerous Veterans' organizations as well as representatives of the City, State and Federal governments.

Since then the *Lexington* has proved to be a major asset to the community. With an annual budget of over $60 million the Museum on the Bay impacts the local economy with an infusion of over $180 million per year. This is accomplished without funds from local, state or federal government agencies—they rely solely on revenues generated from grants, donations, admissions, ship's store sales, special events, and the youth overnight program (which more than a quarter-million participants in the first 20 years). This self-sufficiency allows the museum to cover all operation and maintenance expenses, care for the 20 aircraft aboard on loan from the National Museum of Naval Aviation, and to fund capital improvements such as providing an air-conditioned event area in Hangar Bay II as well as air-conditioned tour routes, and a state-of-the-art 3-D Giant Screen Theater located in the ship's main elevator.

Revenue to both the museum and the city also comes from the continued tradition of Hollywood using the *Lexington* in productions. In her active duty days she appeared on the big screen in "Midway" in 1976, as well as the small screen with "Bob Hope's High-Flying Birthday" (which coincided with the 75th Naval Aviation Anniversary) in 1986, and then by "War and Remembrance" which was filmed not long after the Bob Hope Special, but didn't air until 1988. After her retirement *Lexington* followed up her cinematic stardom with small screen parts in the "JAG" pilot in 1995, "Ghost Hunters" in 2007, and Discovery Channel's "Ghost Lab" in 2009. She was also featured in another big screen appearance as a Japanese carrier in "Pearl Harbor" in 2001.

Seventy years have passed since the *USS Lexington* was launched. Seventy years that have seen war and peace, tragedy and triumph, changing missions and missions accomplished, and service and retirement. Yet, despite her retirement, *Lexington* stills serves. In the twenty-plus years since she embarked on her latest mission, the people now responsible for *Lady Lex* have successfully met the goals set out for her when she was eased into her last berth. First and foremost among those was to preserve for future generations the nation's longest serving and most historically significant *Essex*-class aircraft carrier, and to establish and maintain a major educational and entertaining museum focusing on naval aviation and the role of the aircraft carrier in the national defense. In addition, in order to improve the quality of life of the community, *The Blue Ghost* became a premier community educational facility in support of science, math, history and geography curricula. Moreover, the Lesson of Patriotism—those displays, ceremonies and educational programs that emphasize the heroism and sacrifice of those who have served our nation in the Navy and the Marine Corps—instill pride and patriotism in the public, particularly the youth. It is a lesson that is a little-taught ethic in today's America and the *USS Lexington* will continue teaching it to future generations.

Preface

The *Blue Ghost, USS Lexington* 1942-1991, traces the evolution of the aircraft carrier CV-16 from its "accidental" birth at Quincy, Massachusetts in 1942 to its final decommissioning at Pensacola, Florida in November 1991. Although based on historic facts, this story of the *USS Lexington* is not intended to be a 100 percent factual historical document, but rather a historiography of the fifth Navy warship to bear the name *Lexington*.

Heartfelt appreciation is extended to all those who assisted with, or supplied, research materials and photographs. The author is particularly grateful to Lt. Maureen Ford, JO2 Kelly Lewis and Airman Randolph A. Smith of the *Lexington* Public Affairs Office and PH1 Janice Gains of the *Lexington* Photo Lab.

In keeping with the historic perspective of this historiography, all quotes by *Lexington* wartime commanding officers are taken from the ship's logs. All time references are military times based on a 24-hour cycle, i.e. 0100 (1 a.m.), 1200 (noon), 2400 (midnight), etc.

Front cover photo and the last four photos of the special color section are courtesy of *USS Lexington* Museum On The Bay. The rest of the pictures in the color section are U.S. Navy/National Archive photos (with original captions when available) from the time when the *USS Lexington* was serving as an auxiliary aircraft landing training ship (AVT 16). Unless otherwise noted, all other photographs used in this publication are official U.S. Navy or National Archive photos.

Chapter One

The War Years

The USS Cabot *under construction at Fore River Shipyard, Quincy, Massachusetts, 1942*

It took more than a month for the news of the May 8, 1942 sinking of the *USS Lexington* (CV-2) to reach the residents of Lexington, Massachusetts. Already caught up in the midst of a sweltering summer heat wave, the news of *Lexington's* demise seemed to increase the temperature, adding to the shock and disbelief of the news from the Pacific. The carrier *Lexington* was more than just another Navy ship. It was a part of the very fiber of this New England community. The good people of Lexington had donated a silver service to the CV-2 and many Lexington residents had helped build the carrier at the Fore River Shipyard in nearby Quincy, Massachusetts seventeen years before.

The tragic news quickly brought a plea from residents of Lexington and Quincy to re-name the *USS Cabot* (CV-16), then being built at Fore River, Lexington. With the enthusiastic support of the community and workers at Bethlehem Steel's Fore River Shipyard, a telegram, dated June 16, 1942 was sent to Secretary of the Navy Frank Knox.

Twenty-three thousand workers at Bethlehem's Fore River Yard where the *Lexington* was built respectfully urge you to give the name *Lexington* to your carrier CV-16. We glory in the achievement of that fine ship, the sacrifice of which to many of us is a personal loss. We pledge our utmost efforts to build ships with all the speed and all the skill in our power. We beg the privilege to produce another *Lexington*.

1

The telegram was signed by W.H. Norton, President, Independent Union of Fore River Workers, and W.G. McDermott, Chairman of Employee Members, War Production Committee.

Secretary Knox was so moved by the request that he immediately consulted with President Franklin D. Roosevelt and wired his approval back that same day, thus giving the go-ahead for a new and fifth warship to be named *Lexington*. With a sense of vengeance, shipyard workers completed the construction of CV-16 a full year ahead of schedule.

On Saturday, September 26, 1942, the first hint of fall was in the air as thousands of Navy personnel (many of them former crew members of CV-2), military and civilian dignitaries, and shipyard workers crowded onto the premises of the bustling Fore River Shipyard for the launching of America's newest carrier. At precisely 1305, Mrs. Theodore D. Robinson, the woman who had sponsored CV-2, smashed a champagne bottle against the bow of CV-16, thus setting the ship which would become known as the *Blue Ghost* on a course that would take nearly a half a century to complete.

Five months later February 17, 1943, *Lexington*—decked out with red, white and blue bunting and with numerous multi-colored signal flags fluttering from her rigging—was placed in commission at Boston. Rear Admiral Frederick C. Sherman, the last commanding officer of CV-2 and keynote speaker for the commissioning of CV-16 said, "Today the new *Lexington* takes up where the old left off. May her career be full of glorious achievement." A few moments later, Captain Felix B. Stump, CV-16's first commanding officer, gave the order to hoist the "Commissioning Pennant."

As the slender, spear-shaped, strip of red, white and blue fabric rippled in the breeze, the *USS Lexington* (CV-16) became a living, breathing creature of the sea with a soul and personality of its own. A sudden gust of wind blowing in from Boston Harbor, caused the gallant lady to strain against her mooring

Naval and government officials crowd into the Fore River, Massachusetts Shipyard for the launching of the Lady Lex

2

lines, as though accentuating her obsession to get underway and seek revenge on those who had killed her namesake.

After a two-month fitting out period at the Boston Navy Ship Yard, *Lady Lex* put to sea for sea trials. On April 23, while streaming off the Virginia Coast, her first air group (Air Group 16) flew aboard. After nearly three weeks of training and flight operations, *Lex-* *ington* returned to Boston to replenish her supplies before departing for her final shakedown cruise.

In mid-July 1943, her shakedown complete and all last minute repairs and adjustments made, *Lexington* departed Norfolk, Virginia, for the Pacific. On August 9, after an uneventful passage through the Panama Canal, the *Lady Lex*—sporting twelve 5"/38-caliber

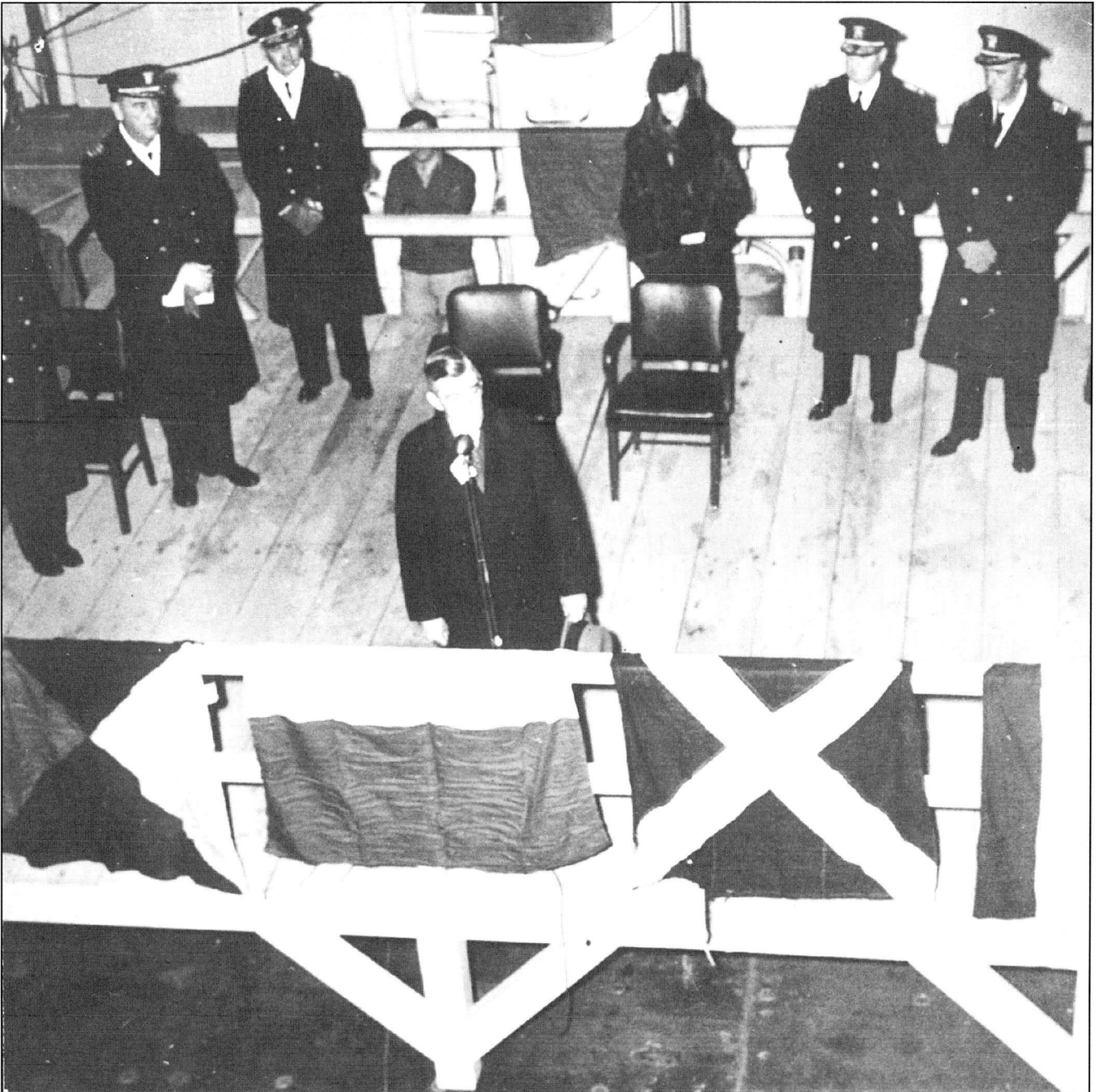

Commissioning of the USS Lexington *(CV-16) at Boston, Massachusetts. Governor L.T. Saltonstall addresses shipyard workers, Naval and government officials and the people of Quincy.*

guns, sixty-eight 40mm and sixty-two 20mm anti-aircraft guns, in addition to Air Group 16—arrived at Pearl Harbor and was assigned to the First Pacific Fleet. A little more than a month later, on September 18, CV-16 got her first taste of combat with a raid on Tarawa.

Late in the day, with most of her aircraft off the deck and en route to the target, *Lexington* sailors got their first real scare of the war. In the ship's dimly-lit Combat Information Center (CIC), a radar operator, staring intently at a small green-colored screen yelled out, "Aircraft bearing 160 degrees. Distance 20 miles and closing." The petty officer of the watch glanced at the clock and calmly noted the time in the ship's log: 1848.

Tension tightened as word of the incoming aircraft quickly spread throughout the 872-foot vessel. Gunners turned their weapons skyward while lookouts strained their eyes staring into the late afternoon haze in a desperate attempt to locate the incoming aircraft. Overhead, the ship's CAP (combat air patrol) assumed a heightened state of alert. With each tick of the clock the aircraft drew closer. Finally, after an agonizing seven minutes, the incoming flight was identified as U.S. torpedo planes returning from a mission.

Similar alarms continued throughout the early evening hours, as friendly aircraft filled the skies en route to and from enemy targets. At 2005, the *Lexington's* first attack group returned to the ship. Pilots reported that although they had encountered very heavy anti-aircraft fire, they had destroyed four seaplanes and left much of the target in flames.

CV-16 slides down the ways at Fore River Shipyard on September 26, 1942.

Shipyard workers cheer the launching of the fifth USS Lexington

Tugs move the Lexington *to an outfitting pier for final outfitting prior to sending the carrier off to war.*

USS Lexington *(CV-16) is launched
a full year ahead of schedule*

USS Lexington *steams through ice in
Boston Harbor, February 17, 1943*

Over the next several hours, *Lexington* aircraft, many riddled by Japanese anti-aircraft fire, continued to find their way back to the ship. By 2336, all aircraft—except one—had returned safely.

With their first combat mission under their belts, tensions eased somewhat. But the ship and her air group remained at a high state of alert as unidentified blips, believed to be Japanese aircraft looking for the *Lexington*, con-

*LSO (Landing Signal Officer) brings a Lexington aircraft aboard (above left). First landing on CV 16
made by Air Group Commander Lt. Cmdr. T.B. Southerland in a F6F-3 (above right).*

6

tinued to appear on the radar screen. After several nerve-wracking minutes, the enemy planes, unable to locate the ship in the inky blackness, retreated back to their base at Tarawa.

Now that she had been tested in battle, the men of *Lexington*, particularly Fighting Sixteen (Air Group 16), were ready and eager for additional combat. They got their wish in early October with a two-day raid on Wake Island. *Lexington* aircraft destroyed or damaged 17 Japanese bombers and 11 other aircraft on the ground while her fighters shot down six enemy planes.

Lexington *departs Norfolk, Virginia for the Pacific, 1943*

A torpedo squadron is maintained by the squadron's mechanics during transit.

7

Lexington *returns to Pearl harbor to prepare for the Gilbert Island's campaign (top left). Carrier Air Group pilots aboard* Lexington *during World War II (top right) Smoke and splashes from two Japanese planes shot down by* Lexington *planes—Gilbert Islands, December 4, 1943 (above).*

Chapter Two

Group photo of Seventh Division taken while Lexington *was in port at Ulithi, November 1944. Notice the Japanese flags, each representing a kill by* Lexington *aircraft, painted on island.*

According to official records, *Lexington* aircraft destroyed a total of 32 enemy aircraft within the first few hours of the raid on Wake. With the Japanese airfields in shambles and nearly three dozen enemy planes burning, the American aircraft returned to their ship. That's not to say *Lexington* airmen escaped completely unscathed, however. According to an entry in the ship's log dated 0320, October 6, 1943, the raid did produce one casualty. A rear-seat gunner was shot in the derriere as his plane was pulling out of a bombing run. To save himself from the inevitable teasing of his shipmates, the unlucky gunner requested that his name be withheld from official records, thus denying himself a certain Purple Heart.

With the first strike group back aboard *Lexington*, Captain Stump addressed the crew. "I'm proud of you all for a job well done," he told the ship's company and air group personnel over the ship's public address system. "We'll stay around and hit them again tomorrow. Be on the alert. We're not in the clear yet."

After a second day of bombing Wake Island, *Lexington* returned to Pearl Harbor to prepare for her next and biggest battle since her entry into the war—the Gilbert Islands.

On November 19, 1943, *Lexington* arrived on station in the Gilberts. Her mission was to provide air cover for the Marines in their attempt to take the islands. At 1835, Captain Stump again addressed the crew. "Last night," he informed the attentive sailors and airmen, "we got word [that] the *Essex* and *Bunker Hill* were being tracked by snoopers [enemy scout planes]. Also, there were enemy planes being grouped for a defense. We know [that] a lot of planes were being landed at Tarawa. We just sent off our attack group for Millie [Atoll]. We expect to hit them all day. This is going to be a long grind," the captain told his men with remorse. "Get as much rest as you can. Do a good job. I will not keep you at GQ (general quarters) longer than necessary. Submarines have been reported in our area, so we can expect a possible torpedo attack sometime tonight. We'll slack off from GQ soon, but first I want to make sure our planes get in and mess Millie up quite a bit. I don't want to be caught with our pants down."

Throughout the reminder of the night and well into the next day, aircraft from *Lexington* and *Yorktown* blasted the island. During the engagement, *Lexington* fighters splashed 17 of 20 enemy planes. On November 28, *Lexington* disengaged from the onslaught of Millie and retired to sea where she rendezvoused with a tanker.

Refueled and replenished with food and munitions, *Lexington* returned to the Marshalls on December 4th for a raid on enemy shipping and aircraft at Kwajalein and Roi. *Lexington* airmen shot down 20 enemy aircraft and destroyed three others on the ground. They then turned their attention to enemy ships, seriously damaging two Japanese cruisers and a cargo vessel.

Lexington *and air group sailors (above) hold a Christmas dance in order to relax prior to a dawn launch (below).*

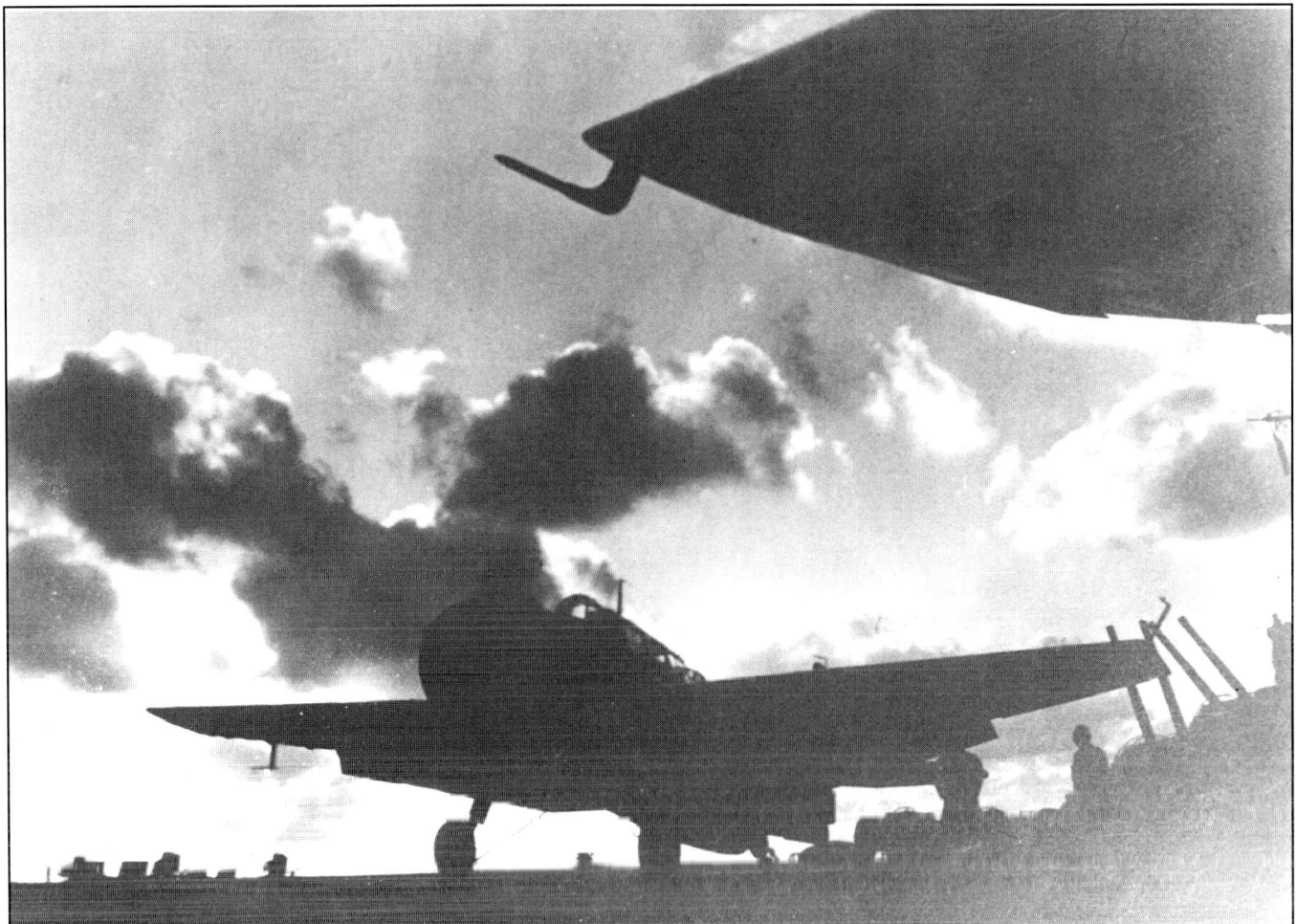

Leaving the airfields at Kwajalein and Roi in ruins and three ships on fire and listing heavily, the *Lexington* birds headed back to the nest. Midway to the ship, *Lexington* dive-bombers were pounced upon by enemy fighters. In a matter of minutes, seven more enemy aircraft, six Zeros (Japanese fighters) and a Betty (twin-engine bomber) had been blasted out of the Pacific skies. Thus far, the *Lady Lex*, although she had been in nearly continuous battle for more than 75 days, had managed to escape the fate of some of her sister ships. That string of luck, however, was about to come to an end.

Around noon on December 4, 1943, *Lexington* came under heavy attack by Japanese torpedo

Japanese aircraft attack USS Lexington *during the Marshall Islands Campaign on December 14, 1943. Photo taken from the deck of the* USS Cowpens *(CV-25).*

planes. Three were shot down by *Lexington* gunners. Several other members of the Emperor's air corps, however, decided it would be best to return and fight another day. One Betty, in making a final pass, came in just above the waves and launched its deadly tin fish. Startled *Lexington* sailors watched anxiously as the sinister wake passed harmlessly astern. While the men of *Lexington* and her air group rejoiced in their good fortune, fate was getting ready to deal a different hand.

At about 1930 numerous bogies appeared on radar screens throughout the task force. The Japanese were closing in for a second attack. As the setting sun gave way to nightfall, anti-aircraft fire from the task force filled the sky. Although the ship had been steaming at a modified battle condition for hours, the general alarm suddenly reverberated throughout *Lexington's* massive hull. From the bridge, Captain Stump could see the deadly barrage take its toll as some enemy planes exploded in the air while others, leaving a fiery wake in the heavens, rocketed toward the inky sea below. Under less serious circumstances the combination of tracers from anti-aircraft guns and brilliant trails of flame shooting through the darkness would have been beautiful.

For more than three hours, *Lexington* gunners fought off wave after wave of determined Japanese pilots. At around 2315, the squawk box (speaker) on the bridge above the captain's head roared to life. "Bogies! 16 miles and closing," the CIC officer informed the skipper.

"Prepare for an a general attack," Captain

Stump calmly told the duty officer, as a burning Japanese plane splashed into the ocean just a few hundred yards off the *Lexington's* port bow.

As Stump skillfully maneuvered the *Lady Lex* through the choppy Pacific waters he could see the anti-aircraft fire from his ship, and other ships of the task force, being reflected in the moonlight. That reflection suddenly became very intense as parachute flares bathed the *Lexington* in an eerie glow. It was now obvious to the men of the *Lexington* as well as the rest of the task force, that the *Lady Lex* was the primary target for the night. As *Lexington* gunners lit up the sky with anti-aircraft fire, a half-dozen or so Japanese planes began a concentrated attack on both sides of the carrier.

Despite the intense, seemly impenetrable, wall of gunfire, a Betty came in from the starboard side, launched its torpedo and roared over the deck and into the night. Seconds later, the torpedo slammed into the ship's starboard side near the chief petty officers' quarters, disabling the steering gear and causing the ship to settle five feet by the stern. Ironically, only minor fires resulted from the explosion and they were quickly brought under control by damage control parties and fire fighting teams. With her steering disabled and her rudder jammed, the mighty flattop began to circle to port, dense-black smoke bellowing from ruptured fuel tanks. To other ships in the task force, viewing *Lexington* through the darkness, the circling, smoking carrier appeared doomed.

At 2336, after receiving damage reports from Damage Control Central and damage control parties scattered throughout the wounded vessel, the

Lexington *damage control personnel make temporary flight deck repairs after a Japanese bomb struck a glancing blow during the battle of the Coral Sea.*

"We're steering by the moonbeam going down the dark side so the bastards can't see us. If we can get by one more hour, we'll be all right, so everyone sit tight. Tomorrow we'll have the other ships around us to shoot down everything that comes at us and we'll be in the clear by tomorrow night."

With the break of dawn, Lexington was gratified to see that the Japanese had left the area and that the ship was out of immediate danger of further attack. Gingerly nursing her wounds, *Lexington* limped back to Pearl Harbor for repairs.

It took marine engineers at Pearl only a few hours to determine that permanent repairs could not be made at what remained of repair facilities at Pearl. A few days later, with emergency repairs complete, *Lexington* refueled, off-loaded most of her aircraft, and got underway for the Naval Shipyard at Bremerton, Washington where permanent repairs to her damaged steering gear could be made.

At about the same time that the wounded carrier was leaving the battle zone, the infamous "Tokyo Rose" reported that the *USS Lexington* had been sunk. This was the first of many such broadcasts reporting the sinking of the *Lexington*, that "Tokyo Rose" would make during the course of the war.

captain addressed the crew. "We have been hit by a torpedo. There is no fire but we have lost steering control. We expect to regain steering soon and I will try and get us to safety. Don't worry!" Stump assured his men.

As the engineers worked feverishly to repair the damage and regain steering control, others summed up the casualties. Two men were dead, seven were missing and 34 were wounded.

After about a half-hour, the ship's engineers, led by Lt. P.N. McDonald and a chief petty officer, had jerry-rigged an emergency hand-operated hydraulic unit and brought the ship's rudder back to mid-ships, thus allowing the carrier to be steered by her engines.

A little past midnight Captain Stump again addressed the crew. "We are in no danger of sinking and we can now do a fair job of steering with the engines," he told them.

Lexington *crew members wipe up oil after a bad landing.*

Chapter Three

After the Marshall Island's Campaign, Lexington *became known as the "*Blue Ghost.*"*

These reports and the fact that *Lexington* was the only *Essex*-class carrier in the Pacific painted a blue-gray rather than with the camouflage pattern of other American capital warships quickly earned her the nickname of *Blue Ghost*.

Despite the fact that December 1943 would be remembered as the month *Lexington* suffered her first major war wound, it was also a blessing in disguise. That wound took her home for the holidays. After an uneventful voyage from Pearl Harbor the *Blue Ghost* arrived at Bremerton Naval Shipyard three days before Christmas.

Hundreds of people, in boats and along the shore of Puget Sound, braved the bitter December cold to cheer the battle-scarred carrier as it slowly inched its way toward the shipyard where anxious workers were waiting to make permanent repairs to her damaged steering gear. Below decks, excited *Lexington* crew members were hastily preparing for their first leave since leaving the States four months earlier.

By the end of February 1944, *Lexington* was back at Pearl Harbor and serving as flag ship for Vice Admiral Marc A. Mitscher's Task Force 58. A week later, *Lexington* returned to her old hunting grounds around Millie Atoll where her air group attacked and destroyed military installations and storage depots. After her "warm-up" against Millie, *Lexington* turned her attention to more worthy targets on Palu and Woleai.

On April 10, 1944, CV-16's first skipper, Captain Felix B. Stump turned command of *Lexington* over to Captain Ernest. W. Litch. Three days later, while supporting Allied landings at Hollanda, Dutch New Guinea, Captain Litch and the *Lexington* crew were surprised to hear "Tokyo Rose" announce—for the second time—that the *Lexington* had been sunk by Japanese bombers.

Encountering only light opposition, *Lexington* remained in the Hollandia area for only a few days of well-deserved R&R before returning to the war. On April 29, 1944, *Lexington*, accompanied by the *USS Enterprise* (CV-6) and the light carrier *San Jacinto* (CVL-30) departed Majuro for the heavily fortified atolls of Truk and Saipan. Nearing Truk, Admiral Mitscher ordered the carriers to launch aircraft.

The first planes were barely off the deck, when two Japanese dive bombers made a high-speed run on *Lexington*. One plane, weaving its way through a hail of anti-aircraft fire, came in low and level from the port beam and released what appeared to be, according to the ship's log, a 250-pound bomb. Fortunately for the *Lady Lex*, the bomb sailed harmlessly over the flight deck. The second plane, striking from the port quarter, exploded in a ball of fire as it ran into a wall of lead spewed skyward by the ship's gunners.

As the air group neared Turk, the Japanese were waiting. Unfortunately for Turk's defenders, the ambush was a complete failure. After several minutes of furious aerial combat, 17 Japanese planes had been splashed by *Lexington* fighters. Sadly, however, the victory was paid for with the loss of four *Lexington* aircraft.

13

Lexington *tailed by one of her destroyer escorts*

Rear Admiral Charles S. Poxnal (at Mike) awards the Distinguished Service Medal to Lexington *Commanding Officer Captain Felix B. Stump.*

Lexington *sailors and air group personnel take time out from their wartime duties to enjoy a few hours liberty on a remote Pacific island.*

When her aircraft were recovered, Mitscher ordered the task force to retire. Again, the infamous "Tokyo Rose" reported that the *Blue Ghost* had been sunk. By now the men of *Lexington* and her air group were beginning to relish their notoriety—*Lexington*, the *Blue Ghost*, the ship which, according to Japan's most famous broadcaster, constantly returned from a watery grave to haunt the Japanese. The next "sinking" would occur a mere two weeks later during the Battle of the Philippine Sea.

The *Lexington's* first strike at Saipan took place at 0328, June 11, 1944. A 200-plane fighter sweep from the task force, designed to reduce air opposition over the target, was launched from approximately 100 miles out. By 0730, reports were filtering back to Mitscher's task force. Although heavy anti-aircraft fire had been encountered, no enemy aircraft had been engaged. With all enemy air opposition eliminated, bombers from *Lexington* and other task force carriers bombed the island at

will for five days.

While the bombers were playing havoc with Saipan, *Lexington* and the task force were being constantly harassed by Japanese torpedo planes based on Guam. Each day it seemed that the attacks grew more intense until, finally on June 15th, radar screens suddenly filled with dozens of bogies, and lookouts shouted excited warnings of large waves of aircraft approaching from the south.

From the ship's log of June 15, 1944:

1907 - Lookouts report planes coming in from the south.
1909 - We have reports 3 twin engine planes coming in dead ahead. Planes coming in off port bow high.
1910 - We have opened fire.
1911 - Planes just made run on the ship. One was seen to have

15

Vice Admiral Marc A. Mitscher, Commander Task Force 58

launched a torpedo.

As lookouts traced the wakes of not one, but two torpedoes, Captain Litch calmly and skillfully maneuvered the *Lexington* between the two torpedoes as they passed harmlessly on either side. Every gun aboard the *Lexington* opened fire nearly simultaneously. The fire was reportedly so furious that at times it completely obscured the view. But one by one the deadly metal birds were dropped into the ocean. One entry in the ship's log reported that a total of seven Japanese bombers were burning at once all around the *Lexington*. In a last desperate attempt to hit *Lexington*, one plane flew the length of the ship's 855-foot flight deck and crashed off the port quarter. Miraculously, despite a lot of shattered nerves, not a single ship was hit. "Tokyo Rose," however, claimed a carrier, the *Lexington*, had been sunk. "This time for keeps," she told her vast audience.

Early the next morning, June 16, 1944, *Lexington* received word that American B-29 bombers were hitting Japan for the first time. A clear indication that the war had truly reached the "Land of the Rising Sun."

Two days later, *Lexington* and the task force steamed westward in search of enemy carriers reportedly approaching the Marianas. The Battle of the Philippine Sea, or the "Marianas Turkey Shoot" as it would come to be known, was about to begin. During the course of the two-day battle, June 19-20, 1944, more than 400 Japanese planes were shot down (45 by *Lexington* airmen). A June 19 log entry made at 2051, summarized the first day of battle:

"The total amount of planes shot down today for the whole force was 284 but we expect to go over the 300 mark before the day is over. We did not contact the Jap carrier force today so we will have to leave that for another day."

The following afternoon, the task force received word that a scout plane had spotted the Japanese carriers some 340 miles to the west. Despite the distance, Admiral Mitscher, from his position in Flag Plot aboard *Lexington*, ordered a launch. When the planes arrived on the scene, they discovered two carriers and several smaller escort ships steaming toward the Marianas. The American aircraft soared in for the attack, their bombs making several direct hits on one of the Japanese flattops which eventually sank, and inflicting heavy damage on several escort ships.

Because of the distance they had to fly to find the target and with daylight quickly fading, time over the targets was limited. With one carrier reported sunk and the other burning, the aircraft broke off the attack and headed back for their respective carriers.

Reaching the task force after dark and low on fuel, the exhausted airmen were forced to land in the water or on whatever carrier was available. Realizing that this melee was claiming more of his aircraft than the Japanese had, Admiral Mitscher, after a great deal of soul searching, ordered the lights of the task force to be turned on so the planes could land. The admiral was well aware that by turning on the lights, he could be committing suicide for the task force.

Mitscher's luck, as it had on numerous occasions during his tenure as Commander Task

Force 58, remained intact. Japanese aircraft had been swept from the skies and if there were any enemy submarines lurking in the area, they failed to take advantage of the situation. With the coming of daylight, Task Force 58 pilots were again in the air searching for the Japanese fleet. But after a day-long search, the airmen were unable to resume contact. *Lexington* and her air group renewed the attacks on the Marianas. After ten days of pounding Japanese targets on Guam, *Lexington* retreated to Eniwetok for some well-earned R&R and a change of air groups.

A chief petty officer strolls down the flight deck of the USS Lexington *during a quiet moment (left).*

The first 5-inch gun crew aboard Lexington *to win the Battle E, May 1943 (right).*

Japanese torpedo bombers are blasted from the skies by Lexington *gunners, December 4, 1943 (below).*

Chapter Four

Vice Admiral Marc A. Mitscher, Commander, Task Force 58 on the bridge of Lexington

On July 9, 1944, with a minimum of pomp and ceremony, Air Group 19 relieved Air Group 16 which had been with the *Lexington* since her sea trials in April 1943. The *Lexington's* ship's company was deeply saddened at the loss of "their" air group. Air Group 16 had been a vital part of *Lexington's* fighting spirit. But after thousands of combat sorties, air group pilots were exhausted, their aircraft worn out or lost to enemy fire. Although they would be missed, *Lexington* crew members were happy that the men of Air Group 16 were finally going home.

A few days later, *Lexington's* props were again churning up the Pacific in support of the Marines efforts to capture Guam. Despite flying more than 550 sorties in support of the Guam landings, and three days of strikes on Palau and Bonins in late July and early August, Air Group 19 encountered no aerial opposition. *Lexington* returned to Eniwetok August 10th, ending her Marianas campaign. The airmen of Air Group 19 were still waiting for their first aerial encounter which was only a little more than three weeks away.

In early September, *Lexington* again put to sea as a member of Admiral William "Bull" Halsey's newly organized Third Fleet and resumed operations in the Philippines in preparation for General Douglas MacArthur's triumphant return. After striking targets at Yap, Ulithi and Mindanao, Air Group 19 finally engaged the enemy in aerial combat over Cebu Island. An entry in the ship's log summarized the activities:

September 14, 1944:

> 0320 - Results of fighter sweep this morning. Fighters hit Cebu north of Mindanao. They found three airfields completely loaded with planes, at least 100. Also many ships of various sizes. They shot down 15 and got 18 more on the ground. By that time they had to leave. Other people are now working them over.

A week later *Lexington* planes struck at Manila doing extensive damage to airfields and leaving the Philippine capital in ruin. The final tally of the

18

Enlisted personnel exercise on flight deck of
USS Lexington enroute to the Gilbert Islands

runs on the Task Force, launching numerous torpedoes which miraculously failed to strike a single ship. Although the Japanese torpedo planes and bombers failed to hit their targets, the relentless attacks did play havoc on the nerves of the *Lexington* crew.

During the daylight hours *Lexington* continued air operations without interference, but as darkness fell, the Japanese returned. Although some hits were recorded on other ships of the task force, *Lady Lex*, as though living up to her *Blue Ghost* nickname, continued to escape undamaged.

At around dawn on October 24th, *Lexington*, steaming east of Luzon was at a high state of readiness. Allied submarines had reported enemy surface forces in the area, but search planes had been unable to locate them. At around 0800 dozens of bogies suddenly appeared on radar. All available aircraft were launched to intercept the on-rushing flock of enemy birds. With the launching of her aircraft, *Lexington* and other units of the task force took advantage of a large rain squall to hide from enemy aircraft while her fighters tried to ward off the attackers. A few Japanese planes did manage to break through the cloud cover, however. And while most were splashed by task force gunners, one managed a direct hit on the light carrier *USS Princeton* (CVL-23). The bomb and her own exploding torpedoes combined to send the *Princeton* to a watery grave.

In the meantime a large enemy force was lo-

attack on Manila by the task force, according to a September 22, 1944 log entry, included 144 Japanese aircraft shot down and 140 destroyed on the ground. *Lexington* aircraft were also instrumental in sinking a destroyer, nine oilers, twenty-five supply vessels, a patrol craft and several barges. Additionally, Air Group 19 put a dry dock out of commission and left docks and shipping facilities at Manila's Clark Field in flames.

Air Group 19 had proven to be aerial warriors of the finest caliber. As a reward for superior performance, *Lexington* and her air group retired to the newly captured Ulithi Atoll in the Western Carolinas for eight days of rest and replenishment.

Her crew rested, her holds again full of provisions and fuel tanks topped off, *Lexington* put to sea again on October 6, 1944 to carry out strikes against Formosa and Okinawa. Unlike earlier engagements at Cebu and Manila, where Air Group 19 roamed pretty much at will, at both Formosa and Okinawa the airmen encountered heavy and determined resistance by the Japanese air force as well as ferocious antiaircraft fire over the target areas.

Nevertheless, the air group knocked down 28 enemy fighters. To counter, the Japanese launched concentrated air strikes against *Lexington* and the task force.

Over the next several days Japanese bombers made dozen of

Lexington sailors and air crews take time out for sporting activities while ship is at anchor at an atoll in the Pacific

19

Lexington *pilots prepare to launch*

four carriers, which had been sighted the day before, were caught with the majority of their planes on deck. Air Group 19 quickly rushed in for the kill. A dozen or more Japanese defenders rose to meet the attacking Americans and were subsequently annihilated.

Wave after wave of American aircraft pounced upon the enemy carriers and their support ships. When the attack concluded several hours later, three carriers—*Chitose*, *Chiyoda* and *Zuikaku*—had been sunk and the fourth, the *Zuiho*, badly damaged. A second strike by planes from the *USS Essex* sank the lone remaining carrier. With the loss of four aircraft carriers in a single battle, the Japanese naval air force had been all but eliminated. But, unbeknown to the men of the *Lexington*, Japan's most deadly weapon—the *Kamikaze* (Divine Wind)—was about to take wing.

In the hours and days following the sinking of the Japanese carriers, one name in particular, *Zuikaku*, was bitter-sweet for the men of the *Lady Lex*. It was the *Zuikaku's* aircraft that had been responsible for the sinking of CV-2. The *Lexington's* namesake had been revenged.

cated in the Sibuyan Sea and all available aircraft were ordered to attack. Air Group 19, joining forces with aircraft from other task force air groups, sank the Japanese battleship *Musashi* and scored direct hits on three Japanese cruisers.

The next day, a Japanese force, including

Lexington *sailors enjoy a Pacific sunset during a lull in the fighting during Marianas Turkey Shoot   June 10, 1944*

Chapter Five

Joyfully the *Lexington* returned to Ulithi for another few days rest before resuming strikes on strongholds in the Philippines. On November 5, 1944, while her aircraft were attacking the Japanese cruiser *Nachi* off Luzon, *Lexington* herself was being attacked. At 1237, according to the ship's log, a lone enemy pilot, determined to crash into the *Lexington*, took deadly aim and began a steep dive. A hail of gunfire from *Lexington* gunners splashed the dive bomber a thousand yards off the ship's bow. But even before the plane had completely broken up a second suicidal flyer took "aim" and managed to release his bomb before crashing into the ship's island structure. *Lexington* had become acquainted with the Divine Wind.

Forty-seven men were killed and 127 wounded. The signal bridge was nearly destroyed and numerous gun emplacements were taken out. Fires erupting as a result of spilled gasoline and exploding ordnance were quickly brought under control by well-trained and determined damage control parties, saving the ship from further damage.

While fire fighters were dousing the flames, other *Lexington* men were below decks searching for casualties, checking for further damage, and extinguishing small fires started by electrical equipment shorting out. Despite the confusion and shock, sailors throughout the ship helped out wherever needed, quickly bringing the wounded man-of-war back to near normal operations.

A short time later Captain Litch addressed the crew: "Today while [we were] making an emergency turn, an enemy plane crashed into the after end of the island on the starboard side. As a result we have lost a lot of fine men and we have many others in serious condition. All we can do is hope to God the doctors down there [in sick bay] can stand up under the strain," he said, the pain of the ordeal plainly apparent in his voice.

"I asked permission to leave to give these men immediate hospitalization," the captain told his men, "but with the military situation as it is, we'll be here tomorrow. We will probably be up all night but don't get discouraged, for those lousy bastards will never lick us. The screen is clear now but we'll no doubt have bogies throughout the night. Thank you."

On November 7th, *Lexington* went alongside the hospital ship *Solace* to transfer her wounded before proceeding on to Ulithi for repairs. While *Lexington* was steaming toward the anchorage at Ulithi, "Tokyo Rose" again announced that the *Blue Ghost* had been sunk. The ship stayed at Ulithi for the remainder of November while repairs

A Japanese torpedo-bomber pilot slumps over a gun tub after crashing his plane into the Lexington.

A 20mm gun tub suffers major damage from a Japanese suicide plane.

were being made. Near the end of the month, Air Group 20 reported aboard to relieve Air Group 19.

On December 11th, *Lexington*—fully repaired and flying the flag of Rear Admiral Gerald F. Bogan, Commander Task Group 58.2—departed Ulithi to resume air strikes in the Luzon area. This time out, however, the enemy wasn't the Japanese, but the weather. Shortly after leaving Ulithi, the *Lexington* task group found itself in the midst of a typhoon. Although the storm severely damaged several smaller ships, *Lexington* rode it out and returned to Ulithi for the holidays. Considering the fact that the ship was thousands of miles from home, Christmas 1944 was nevertheless a joyful one. With little danger of being attacked from sky or sea, the men of the *Lexington* and Air Group 20 basked in the sun, sang Christmas carols, played baseball, listened to Glenn Miller on Armed Forces Radio and exchanged gifts. The

war—at least for a short while—was a long way off.

All too soon, however, it was back to business. The first couple of weeks in January 1945 found *Lexington* airmen flying missions against targets on Luzon and Formosa.

Lexington next entered the South China Sea where she hit the enemy in Vietnam and Hong Kong. On January 27th, *Lexington* returned to Ulithi for a double change of command.

On January 30th, Captain Thomas H. Robbins relieved Captain Litch as skipper of the *Lexington* and Rear Admiral Ralph E. Davison relieved Rear Admiral Bogan as Commander of Task Group 58.2. Two days later, February 1, 1945, Air Group 9 replaced Air Group 20.

On February 10, 1945, the *Blue Ghost* departed her anchorage at Ulithi for what would be her last major engagement of the war—providing air cover for the invasion and capture of Iwo Jima and attacks on Tokyo itself. On the fifteenth, Captain Robbins informed the crew of the Task Force's mission: "I want to give you an idea of what will take place tomorrow and the next day. At dawn tomorrow we will be just off the coast of Japan. Our air groups will take off for targets in the vicinity of Tokyo. Air Group 9 has been assigned 16 airfields, including the finest one in Japan—in the heart of Tokyo. This isn't a rush affair, but a highly thought-out plan on the road to victory.

"As the operation goes on I or the exec will relay to you all possible information. In a matter of a few days you will see how this scheme progresses. We don't expect the Japanese to take this laying down. The going might get tough so I want everyone to do his job just a little bit better than before.

"This is what we have all been waiting for and when every plane takes off we can truly say, "DESTINATION TOKYO!"

For the next few days Air Group 9 pounded targets in and around Tokyo despite heavy cloud cover which greatly reduced visibility. The bad weather not only bene-fitted the Japanese, it also limited Japanese opposition against the air group. Neverthe-less, by the time *Lexing-ton* departed the area, Air Group 9 had shot down 25 Japanese planes and destroyed another 18 on the ground.

Lexington returned to the Tokyo area on February 23rd only to find the target totally obscured by foul weath-er. Unable to find suita-ble targets, the task force withdrew from the area and returned to Ulithi. Good news awaited *Lady Lex*. After more than a year in the battle zone, the *Blue Ghost* was going home for an overhaul. During the next few days, Air

Repair crews make temporary repairs following an enemy attack.

Group 9 was transferred and Air Group 3—also returning to the States—reported aboard.

Departing Ulithi March 7, 1945, *Lexington* lift-ed anchor and set a course for the West Coast of the United States. Twenty-four days later she en-

Christmas services aboard the Blue Ghost *in the Pacific*

tered the Puget Sound Naval Shipyard at Bremer-ton, Washington.

Lexington's return home at this particular time was more of a blessing then anyone aboard could have possibility imagined. It was during the three months she was away from the battle zone, that the American fleet endured Japan's most ferocious *Kamikaze* onslaught. While the *Blue Ghost* was in the yards, Japan's deadly Divine Wind was raining down on the battle-weary flattops, inflicting heavy damage on the carriers *Franklin*, *Intrepid*, *Enterprise*, *Bunker Hill* and dozens of other American warships. The luck of the *Lady Lex*, the acci-dental carrier, was working over-time.

By mid-May, overhaul com-plete, *Lexington* left Bremerton for a short stopover at Alameda, Cali-fornia where she completed re-plenishment and welcomed aboard a number of new crew members and passengers, before setting sail for the western Pacific and her third and final combat cruise.

23

F6F-3 Hellcat lands during the Battle of the Philippine Sea, June 1944.

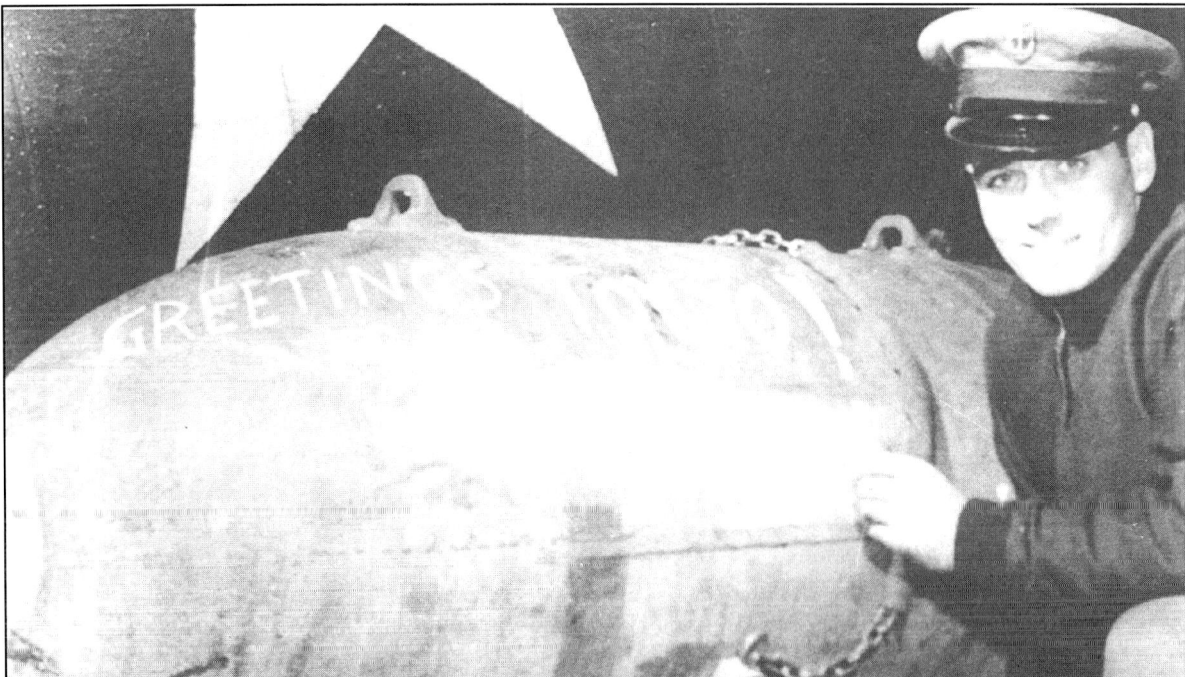

A Lexington chief petty officer (left) prepares a gift for Tokyo from his wife, Mildred.

Lexington and Air Group chief petty officers relax over an evening meal (top right).
A Japanese pilot, rescued after his plane was shot down, joins an American Naval officer in giving the "V" for victory sign from his bunk in Lexington's *sick bay (center right).*
Lexington *sailors and airmen react to the news that the war is nearly over— June 1945 (bottom right).*

Arriving at Pearl Harbor at the end of May, *Lexington* welcomed Air Group 94 and a squadron of Corsairs aboard and immediately put to sea for a week of training exercises. Although many of her combat-hardened veterans were still aboard, their wartime edge had dulled during their three-month yard period in the States.

Satisfied, after several days of intensive drills, that his crew was once again combat ready, Captain Robbins got underway for Leyte where he laid at anchor until July 1st.

As the boatswain's mates hoisted anchor that hot humid July day, never in their wildest imagination would they have dared imagine that the next time they released the 15-ton hook that it would be smack-dab in the middle of Tokyo Bay.

For the remainder of July 1945, *Lexington* and Air Group 94 conducted air strikes at the very heart of the Japanese mainland with little opposition from Japanese aircraft. On July 30th, while steaming northward toward the island of Honshu, *Lexington*—along with the rest of the world—learned that an atomic bomb had been dropped on Hiroshima. Although most of the ship's company had never heard of Hiroshima or the atomic bomb, the undisputed announcement that a single bomb had completely destroyed a major city left little doubt in their minds that the war was nearly over.

MISSIONARIES" McLELLAN, HUTCHINSON AND GREENHALGH EARN MEMBERSHIP BY SHOWING HOW THEY BLEW UP 16 JAP CRUISERS AND THREE CARRIERS FROM RUBBER BOAT

Life Goes to an Aircraft-Carrier Party

Officers and crew of a flat top form the "West of Tokyo Missionary Society" to commemorate the bombing of Palau

The "West of Tokyo Missionary Society" was founded somewhere in the Pacific Ocean by the crew of a aircraft carrier who wanted to commemorate the Navy's first attack on Jap positions west of Tokyo successful smashing of Palau Island last March. The raiders' righteous purpose, as set down in their high-sounding "manifesto," was to celebrate this "zealous attempt to convert the reluctant and retiring Japanese

fleet." The "missionaries," declared the manifesto, "by their enlightening bombs converted over 30 heathen ships—to scrap iron."

The missionary society's behavior was a lot less solemn than its language. Its one big meeting on the carrier, recorded by LIFE's Photographer J. R. Eyerman, was devoted to flat-top horseplay. A hierarchy of high-pressure, ministering and honorary missionaries was es-

tablished. Some applicant missionaries were forced to re-enact tall tales of shooting Japs down from rubber boats or tearing enemy planes apart with bare hands. The whole membership, which included the crew and the task force's admiral, had to take an oath promising to have nothing to do with whisky or women while aboard ship— a display of mock saintliness since neither temptation is available on U. S. Navy aircraft carriers.

The committee on rules worked hard on the charter. But at the first meeting vociferous members society forced through an amendment to provide for "proper refreshments and amusements."

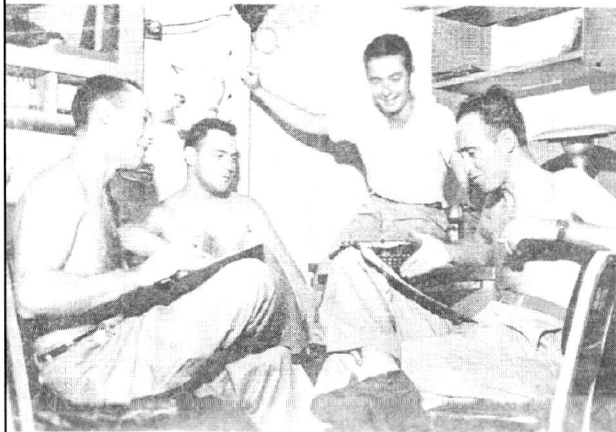

The committee on credentials decided whether the applicants were to be high-pressure missionaries, mostly fliers, or ministering missionaries, mostly nonflying crew members.

Chapter Six

Lexington *crewmembers prepare to load bombs on aircraft.*

During the next two weeks, as the Japanese debated surrender terms, *Lexington* airmen continued their attacks against airfields and shipping in the area around Honshu. They then turned their attention to the industrial targets of Tokyo. Air strikes over Japan's largest city were now considered little more than milk runs. *Lexington* airmen could launch, fly to the target, drop their bombs and return without the slightest interference from Japanese aircraft.

On August 15th, one attack against the industrial city of Hyakurigahara had been completed and a second wave of *Lexington* aircraft were midway to the target when the strike commander was ordered to suspend operations and return to the ship. The Japanese had agreed to surrender. The war was over!

Moving to within 100 miles of the coast of Honshu Island, the *Lady Lex*, on August 25, 1945, began a series of flights to locate POW camps. On the first mission, Air Group 94 pilots discovered five camps, each plainly marked with huge "PW" letters. Going in low for a closer look, the airmen were greeted with the jubilant dancing and waving of Allied prisoners of war. Within a matter of hours, *Lexington* had launched a "mercy flight" laden with more than a thousand pounds of supplies—toilet articles, food, clothing, magazines, and a specially printed edition of the *Lexington's* daily newspaper, *The Sunrise Press*.

On September 5, 1945, *Lexington* sailed into

Tokyo Bay and dropped anchor. The *Blue Ghost*, the carrier "Tokyo Rose" had reported time and again to have been sunk, was the first carrier to enter Tokyo Bay.

For *Lexington* the battle—which had started at Tarawa nearly two years earlier—was over, but her services were still in demand. For the next two months *Lexington* airmen continued to drop supplies to POW camps and fly precautionary patrols for the occupation of Japan. On November 18th, Captain B.E. Grow assumed command and prepared to return to the States.

On December 3, 1945, with hundreds of returning GIs jammed into her hangar bays and taking up refuge on her flight deck, *Lexington* boatswain's mates hoisted anchor and the *Lady Lex* steamed out of Tokyo Bay en route to San Francisco. *Lexington* had spent a total of 21 months in actual combat. Her aircraft were responsible for the destruction of 1,022 enemy aircraft—387 in the air and 635 on the ground. *Lexington's* air groups sank more than 300,000 tons of Japanese shipping and damaged an additional 600,000 tons. The gunners aboard the *Blue Ghost* had shot down 15 Japanese aircraft and assisted in downing five others.

Born by accident, the result of a demand by the people of Lexington and Quincy, Massachusetts to send another *Lexington* to war to avenge the loss of CV-2, the *Blue Ghost*—her mission accomplished—majestically sailed under the Golden Gate Bridge on December 15, 1945. The battle-hardened pride of Lexington, Massachusetts, sent in harm's way to avenge her namesake, had returned home triumphantly. More than 5,000 men served aboard *Lexington* during War World II and all but 245 returned at war's end.

For her wartime service, *Lexington* was awarded 11 battle stars and a Presidential Unit Citation. Only two other carriers earned more battle stars than *Lexington*—the *USS Enterprise* (20) and the *USS Essex* (13). Additionally, *Lexington* was one of only six carriers to win the prestigious Presidential Unit Citation.

On October 11, 1946, the *Lady Lex* was taken out of service and placed in the Reserve Fleet at Bremerton, Washington.

Lexington *and her escort ships return to the United States at war's end.*

THE SECRETARY OF THE NAVY

WASHINGTON

The President of the United States takes pleasure in presenting the PRESIDENTIAL UNIT CITATION to the

U.S.S. LEXINGTON

and her attached Air Groups participating in the following operations:

September 18, 1943, Tarawa; October 5-6, 1943, Wake; November 19 to December 5, 1943, Gilberts: AG-16 (VF-16, VB-16, VT-16).

March 18 to April 30, 1944, Palau, Hollandia, Truk; June 11 to July 5, 1944, Marianas: AG-16 (VF-16, VB-16, VT-16, Part of VFN-76).

July 18 to August 5, 1944, Marianas, Palau, Bonins; September 6 to November 6, 1944, Philippines, Palau, Yap, Ryukyus, Formosa, Luzon: AG-19 (VF-19, VB-19, VT-19, Part of VFN-76).

December 14-16, 1944, Luzon; January 3 to 22, 1945, Philippines, Formosa, China Sea, Ryukyus: AG-20 (VF-20, VB-20, VT-20).

February 16 to March 1, 1945, Japan, Bonins, Ryukyus: AG-9 (VF-9, VBF-9, VB-9, VT-9).

June 20, 1945, Wake; July 10 to August 15, 1945, Japan: AG-94 (VF-94, VBF-94, VB-94, VT-94).

for service as set forth in the following

CITATION:

"For extraordinary heroism in action against enemy Japanese forces in the air, ashore and afloat in the Pacific War Area from September 18, 1943, to August 15, 1945. Spearheading our concentrated carrier-warfare in the most forward areas, the U.S.S. LEXINGTON and her air groups struck crushing blows toward annihilating Japanese fighting power; they provided air cover for our amphibious forces; they fiercely countered the enemy's aerial attacks and destroyed his planes; and they inflicted terrific losses on the Japanese in Fleet and merchant marine units sunk or damaged. Daring and dependable in combat, the LEXINGTON with her gallant officers and men rendered loyal service in achieving the ultimate defeat of the Japanese Empire."

For the President,

James Forrestal
Secretary of the Navy

C-73249

F6F goes down deck for take-off from the USS Lexington

Crewmen hastily drag plane with
flat tire down flight deck to make
way for next plane to land

Missed arrestor cable while trying to land, May 21, 1943

Enlisted men relaxing on flight deck

*Pilots leaning across a F6F on board celebrate after shooting
down 17 out of 20 Japanese planes heading for Tarawa*

*Crewmen laughing as they listen to pilots
humorously describe encounter with Japanese planes over the ship's bullhorn*

Ratings

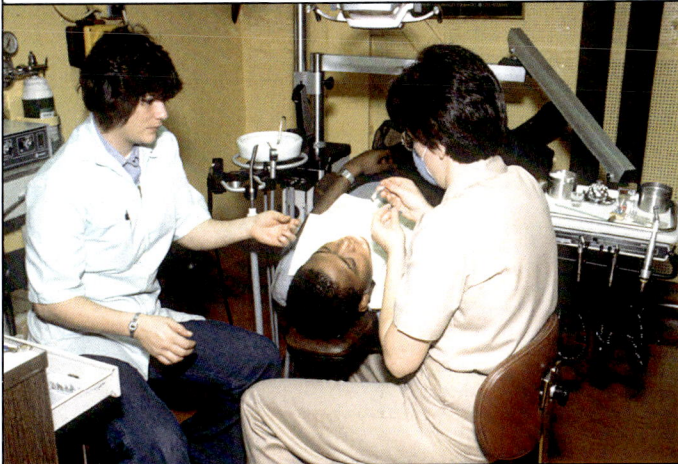

Dentist LT. Elaine R. Winegard (right) treats a patient with assistance from a dental technician

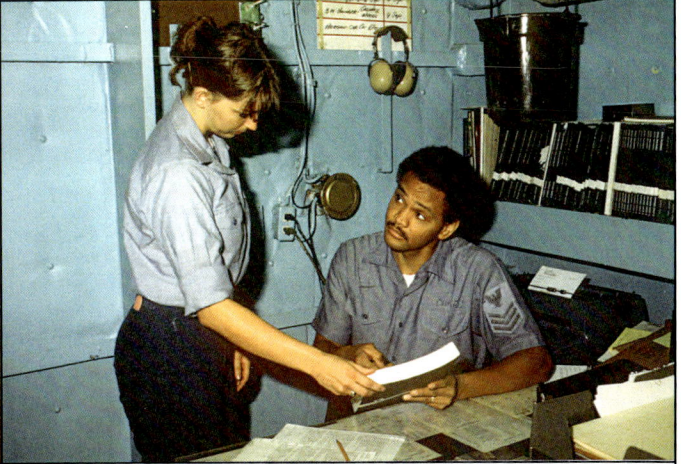

Personnelman 1ST Class Donald Dukes gives assistance to Fireman Kathleen A. McGough

Religious Program SPECIALIST 3rd Class Diane R. Maroon files books in the library

A crash crewman, wearing a fire retardant suit, stands by on the flight deck

In the flight operations center aboard the training ship, the "mini boss" assists the air officer in directing flight operations in the Gulf of Mexico

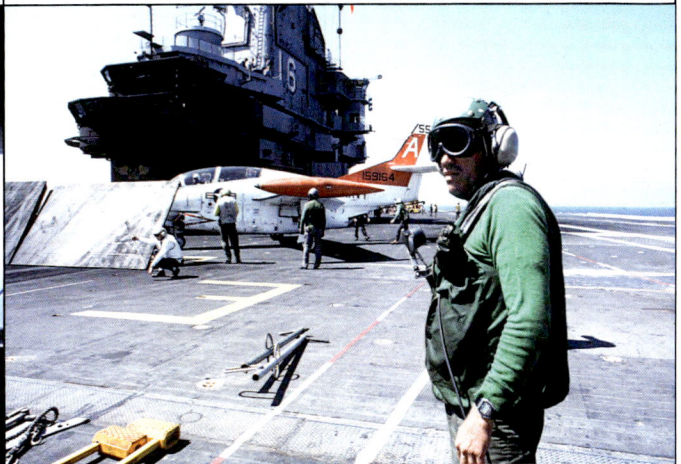

Flight deck crewman checks preparations to launch one aircraft while a T-2C Buckeye aircraft waits behind the blast deflector for its turn at the catapult

Yeoman 1ST Class Tonya Skipper performs clerical duties in the captian's office

Kim Mattorochia, a hospital corpsman striker, files medical records in the dispensary

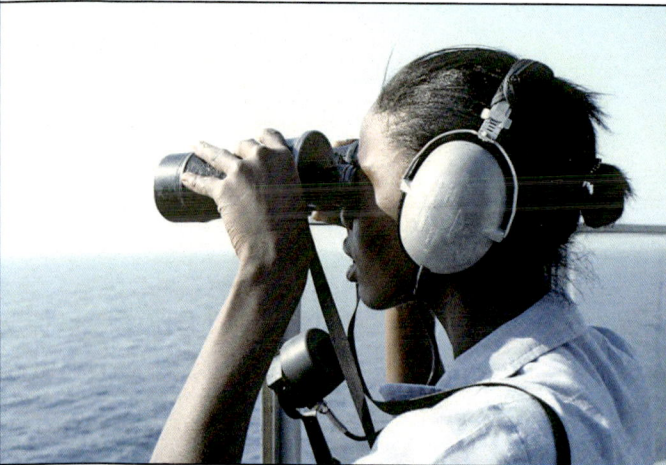

SEAMAN Robin P. Robinson, equipped with binoculars and a sound-powered phone set, performs lookout duties aboard the USS LEXINGTON

An electronics technician works on the mast aboard the training carrier. The ship's SPS-10 surface search radar antenna is visible in the background

Journalist SEAMAN Sheila Heaphy performs public relations duties in an office aboard the training aircraft carrier USS LEXINGTON (AVT-16)

In the flight operations center, a petty officer makes an entry on a log sheet as he observes the activities in progress on the flight deck during pilot training

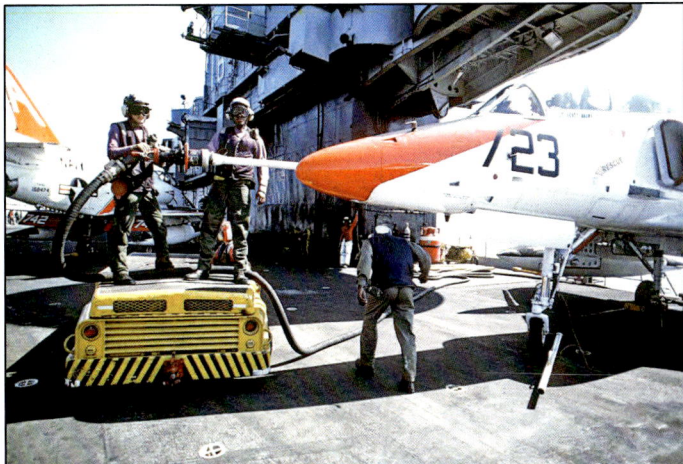

Two crewmen stand atop an MD-3A tow tractor as they refuel a TA-4J Skyhawk aircraft

A landing signal officer (LSO) on the flight deck signals a wave off to an incoming student pilot

A crewman using a tow bar hauls a TA-4J Skyhawk toward a parking spot on the flight deck during pilot carrier training

A catapult officer signals for the launch of a Training Squadron 21 (VT-21) TA-4J Skyhawk aircraft on the flight deck

A hook runner stands ready to disengage the crossdeck pendant from the tailhook of a T-2C Buckeye aircraft on the flight deck

The safety leading chief petty officer keeps a close eye on the aircraft launch and recovery activities on the flight deck during pilot carrier training

Bob Hope's Celebration of the 75th Anniversary of Naval Aviation USO Show

Entertainer Bob Hope hosts a USO show aboard the training aircraft carrier USS LEXINGTON during the celebration of the 75th anniversary of Naval Aviation

Entertainers Bob Hope and Jonathan Winters perform in a USO show during the celebration of the 75th anniversary of Naval Aviation

Entertainers Bob Hope, Sammy Davis, Jr., and Jonathan Winters perform their impression of the Andrew Sisters in a USO show aboard the carrier

Entertainers Phylicia Rashad, Barbara Mandrell and Brooke Shields perform in a United Service Organization (USO) show aboard the USS LEXINGTON

Bob 'Swabbie' Hope is "woman-handled" by Barbara Mandrell, Phylicia Rashad, and Brooke Shields

Entertainers Mac Davis, Bob Hope and Sammy Davis Jr. perform in the USO show

Bob Hope introduces Elizabeth Taylor during the celebration of the 75th anniversary of naval aviation

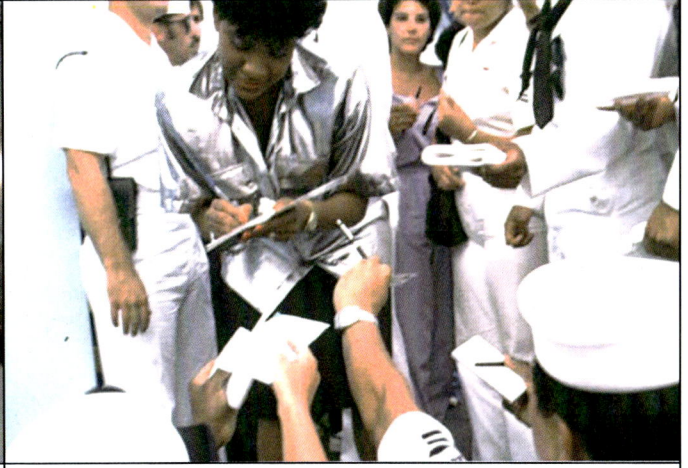

After her performance Phylicia Rashad returned to the stage and signed autographs for nearly an hour

60 year-old Sammy Davis, Jr. (left) performs in the USO show aboard the training aircraft carrier during the celebration of the 75th anniversary of naval aviation. He is joined onstage by Bob Hope (center), who would be celebrating his 83rd birthday later that month. Phylicia Rashad (right) performs a solo in the USO show

Some crewmembers fill in as extras in skits, most officers and sailors enjoy the show from the flight deck with Secretary of the Navy John F. Lehman

At the end of the show, Bob Hope was presented with a 75th Naval Aviation Anniversary plaque Rear Admiral John S, Disher, Chief of Naval Air Training

Filming "War and Remembrance"

Actors in World War II aviator uniforms take direction from atop an SNJ Texan aircraft parked on the deck

Special effects crew fires a Mark 4 20 mm anti-aircraft gun installed aboard the carrier

A line of World War II-era bombs are staged on the flight deck during filming of the ABC-TV movie "War and Remembrance." An SNJ Texan aircraft (left), and an F4F Wildcat aircraft are in the background

Clips of ammunition fill the breech mechanism of a twin 40 mm Bofors gun mount installed on the carrier during filming of the movie. Actors are working on an SNJ Texan aircraft in the background

An SNJ Texan aircraft is pushed onto the flight deck of the training aircraft carrier USS LEXINGTON

World War II-era aircraft fill the flight deck for the filming. Seen here are SNJ Texans and F4F Wildcats

The USS LEXINGTON *portrayed both the* USS Yorktown *and the* USS Enterprise, *as well as Japan's* IJN Akagi—*which aircraft from the* Lexington *actually attacked during World War II. Hundreds of* Lexington *sailors and service members from Pensacola Naval Air Station were cast in bit parts by the producers of the movie*

Operations and Events

Right side view of a C-1 Trader aircraft from Fleet Logistic Support Squadron 40 (VRC 40)

A catapult officer signals to launch an A-6 Intruder aircraft from the training aircraft carrier

A TH-57 Sea Ranger helicopter lands on the deck of the USS LEXINGTON *during helicopter flight training*

A-7 Corsair II aircraft parked on the flight deck, framing the ship's bridge in the background

A pair of T-2C Buckeyes aircraft wait behind the blast deflector for their turns at the catapult. At upper right are parked a C-2A Greyhound aircraft and a Coast Guard HH-65A Dolphin helicopter

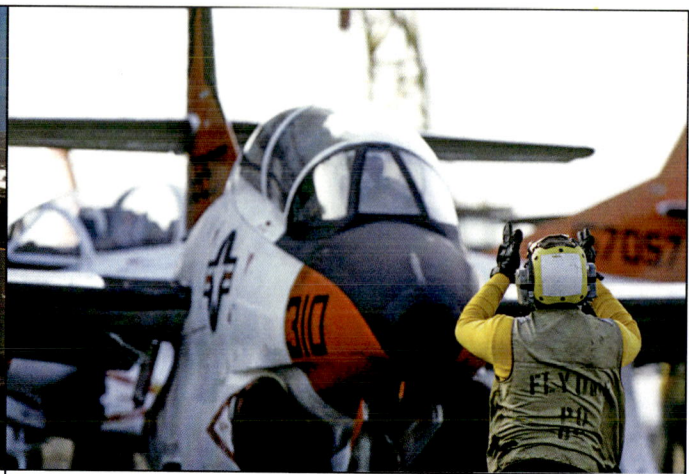

A plane handler guides the pilot of a taxiing T-2C Buckeye aircraft forward toward a catapult on the flight deck of the USS LEXINGTON during pilot carrier training in the Gulf of Mexico

A starboard bow view of the auxiliary aircraft landing training ship USS LEXINGTON (AVT-16) underway as it departs from the naval station

A crewman attaches a tow bar to the nose gear of a TA-4J Skyhawk aircraft on the flight deck as a plane handler signals to other members of the flight deck crew during pilot carrier training in the Gulf of Mexico

A TA-4J Skyhawk aircraft waits behind the blast deflector for its turn at the catapult as another Skyhawk begins to climb after being launched from the flight deck during pilot carrier training

Two flight deck crewmen rush to retrieve a catapult bridle used in the launch of the T-2C Buckeye aircraft that has just left the flight deck of the USS LEXINGTON in the Gulf of Mexico

A T-2C Buckeye aircraft approaches to land aboard the training aircraft carrier, while two other T-2 aircraft are visible on the flight deck

A TA-4J Skyhawk aircraft is catapulted from the training aircraft carrier USS LEXINGTON (AVT 16)

The tailhook on a TA-4J Skyhawk about to catch the arresting wire on the flight deck of the auxiliary aircraft landing training ship USS LEXINGTON

A TA-4J Skyhawk aircraft from Training Wing 2 (TW-2) catches an arresting wire on the flight deck of the auxiliary aircraft landing training ship

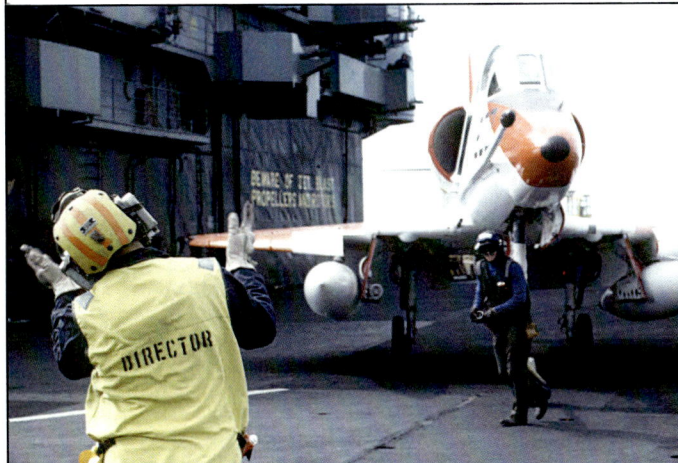

A plane director guides a student through the paces of flight deck operations aboard the aircraft carrier. The aircraft being used is a TA-4J Skyhawk

A CH-46 Sea Knight helicopter from Helicopter Combat Support Squadron 16 (HC-16) hovers above the training carrier during a search and rescue mission

A PBY Catalina aircraft over USS LEXINGTON at Naval Air Station, Pensacola, during the celebration of the 75th anniversary of naval aviation

The landing site and headquarters for Exercise AGILE SWORD '86 with the auxiliary aircraft landing training ship USS LEXINGTON in the background

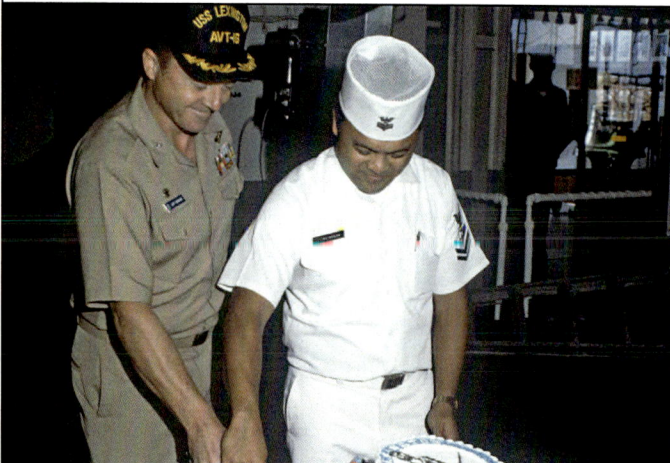
Captain H. J. Bernsen, commanding officer of the USS LEXINGTON, cuts a cake with the assistance of Mess Management SPECIALIST First Class Serafin Apongan to celebrate the Navy's 208th birthday

A pilot surveys a wing embedded in the superstructure of the USS LEXINGTON. A T-2C Buckeye aircraft crashed into the ship on October 29 during routine training, killing five people and injuring 19

LT. Patricia A. Denkler of VT- 4 became the first woman to be carrier qualified in a jet aircraft when she landed aboard the USS LEXINGTON September 1981. A year later, and now Patricia Denkler Rainey, she was the first woman to land an A-6 on a carrier

The 493,760th—and last—arrested landing aboard the carrier USS LEXINGTON was made by a C-2 Greyhound cargo plane from VRC-40. It was piloted by Lt. Cathy Owens and her crew, Lt. Paul Villagomez (copilot) and Petty Officer Danny Kicklighter

Capt. William H. Kennedy (left), Lexington's 33rd and final skipper, reported aboard on December 18, 1990. The next month AVT-16 went to sea for the last time

The world-famous Blue Angels, returning to their home base at NAS Pensacola, make an approach on the Lexington operating in the Gulf of Mexico

A sailor flashes a smile as crew members man the rails on the flight deck as the LEXINGTON moved its home from NAS Pensacola to the Port of Pensacola, from which it operated until replaced

Crew members man the rails of the USS LEXING-TON as a tug moves into position to help it dock at its new home in the Port of Pensacola from which it operated until replace by the USS KITTY HAWK

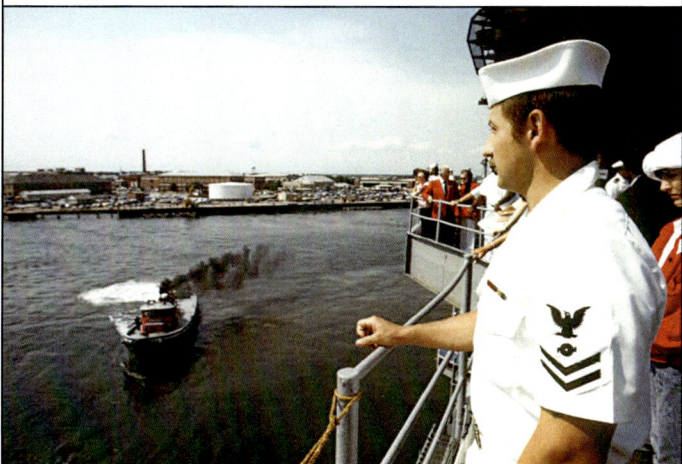

A petty officer standing on a catwalk on board the USS LEXINGTON as a tug approaches to help the ship dock at its new home in the Port of Pensacola

AIRMAN Apprentice Michael Pando, a crewman aboard the auxiliary aircraft landing training ship, embraces his girlfriend on the pier

Despite a bitter-cold day, more than 4,000 people were on hand for the decommissioning of the Lady Lex *on November 8, 1991*

As the Lady Lex *left the Cradle of Naval Aviation for the last time, Lt. Laura Wolfgang donned a mermaid suit to bid bon voyage*

USS LEXINGTON Museum On The Bay

Lady Lex, *the* Blue Ghost *of the Gulf Coast, now proudly serves as the* USS LEXINGTON *Museum On The Bay at Corpus Christi, Texas*

Naval training aircraft perform a flyover at the USS LEXINGTON *Museum On The Bay*

Naval aircraft on static display line the flight deck of the USS LEXINGTON *Museum On The Bay*

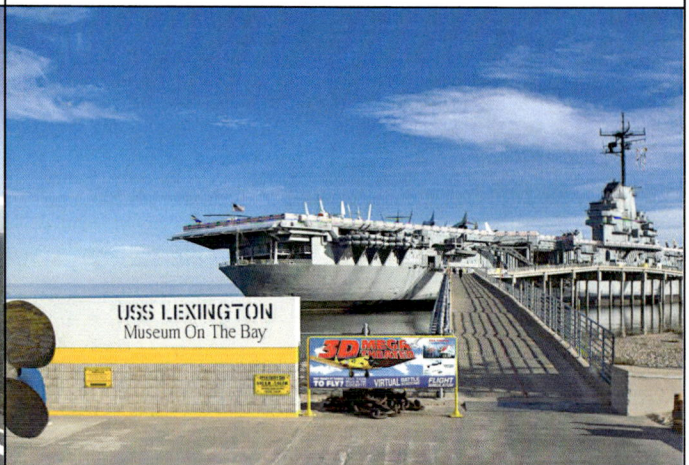
Entrance to the USS LEXINGTON *Museum On The Bay at Corpus Christi, Texas*

Chapter Seven

Although deserving of a long rest, the outbreak of the Korean War in 1950, and other world-wide communist threats combined to give *Lexington* a new lease on life. In October 1952, while still a part of the United States Naval Reserve Fleet, the Navy redesignated *Lexington*, and her *Essex*-class sisters, as CVAs (attack carriers). Eleven months later, September 1, 1953, *Lexington* entered drydock for a major conversion.

Two years later, *Lexington* emerged from drydock, bearing little resemblance to the battle-scarred flattop "Tokyo Rose" had dubbed the *Blue Ghost*. CVA-16 sported an angled deck, steam catapults and an enclosed "hurricane" bow. Her island structure had been strengthened and the crews' quarters and work stations had been redesigned and air conditioned with crew comfort in mind. Her five-inch gun mounts had been removed and the number three elevator replaced by a starboard deck-edge elevator. The new *Lexington* had also gained weight during her two years in the yards. When she was commissioned in 1942, *Lexington* displaced 34,000 tons. After conversation she displaced 42,000 tons.

The *Lady Lex* that Captain Alexander S. Hayward, Jr. recommissioned on August 15, 1955 was for all intents and purposes, a brand new carrier. After a shakedown cruise off the coast of Southern California, *Lexington* sailed into her new home port of San Diego, California in early March 1956. The *Blue Ghost* was back and ready to resume her role as part of the mighty U.S. Pacific Fleet. In the spring of 1956, the newly converted attack carrier departed San Diego for her first Far East deployment since recommissioning. *Lexington's* air group included attack planes armed with Bullpup guided missiles, the first air-to-surface missiles to be deployed aboard a carrier.

Throughout the remainder of the 1950s, *Lexington* returned time and again to her wartime operating areas around Okinawa, the Philippines, Hong Kong, Formosa, Vietnam and Japan as part of the U.S. Seventh Fleet. Ironically, during her tenure with the Seventh Fleet, *Lexington*, the wartime antagonist of the Imperial Japanese Navy made her overseas home at the sprawling World II Japanese Naval Base at Yokosuka, Japan.

While the *Lexington* was enjoying a new lease on life, the Navy's only training carrier—the Pensacola-based *USS Antietam* (CVS-36)—was nearing the end of her useful life. Her power plant beyond repair and her flight deck too small and weak to handle modern fleet aircraft, the Navy Department decided it was time for *Antietam* to retire. In January 1962, *Lexington* skipper Captain Hart D. Hilton was notified that *Lexington* was being reassigned to the Atlantic Fleet as the eventual replacement for the *USS Antietam*. Six months later, July 23, 1962, the *Lady Lex*—with new commanding officer Captain Lucien C. Powell at the helm—eased away from her San Diego berth and began a 15,000-mile journey around Cape Horn to New York where she was to be overhauled before assuming her new role as the Navy's training aircraft carrier.

Throughout her service life, in war and peace, *Lexington* had sailed on the edge, so to speak. It was therefore no surprise that she became the first carrier to conduct flight operations in the storm-prone area of Cape Horn at the tip of South America during the transit from Pacific to Atlantic. *Lexington's* role as a fleet battle carrier may have been coming to a end, but the number of "firsts" she would achieve over the next two decades was just beginning.

Upon arrival at the New York Naval Ship-yard, workmen swarmed over her flight deck, hangar decks and engineering spaces, preparing her for her new role as a training vessel. As the sweltering New York heat gave way to the crispness of autumn and the surrounding country side began its annual metamorphosis, *Lexington* too was being changed. Guns and other war-fighting equipment were being removed and her flight deck strengthened. On October 1, 1962 her designation was changed from CVA to CVS (Anti-Submarine Support Carrier).

CVS-16 was scheduled to relieve the *USS Antietam* at Pensacola in mid-November 1962. But reports of ICBM launch sites being established by the Soviet Union in Cuba, prompted President John F. Kennedy to establish a blockade of the island nation.

With two weeks of her yard period remaining, Captain Powell received unexpected orders to postpone all further work and get underway for Norfolk, Virginia where *Lexington* was to load ammunition and take an air group aboard.

Replenished and with her assigned air group ready for any eventuality, *Lexington* sailed out of Norfolk in mid-October for her port of operations at

USS Lexington *arriving in San Francisco Bay, 1958*

44

A post-World War II Lexington *conducts maneuvers with two other aircraft carriers*

Mayport, Florida. For several tension-filled days, *Lexington* conducted air operations in the "Jacksonville operating area," positioned so that her air group, if needed, could strike Cuban targets in less than 40 minutes.

When the crisis eased, *Lexington* was released to comply with her original orders. Prior to leaving her operating area, the *Blue Ghost* had one final chore to carry out—paying tribute to an accompanying ship. For the duration of the Cuban Missile Crisis, the Mayport-based destroyer *USS Zellers* (DD-777) had performed plane guard duty for *Lexington*. Captain Powell knew that *Zellers* had just returned from a six-month deployment to the Mediterranean when she was ordered to sea for the blockade, despite the fact that nearly half of her crew were on leave.

As *Lexington* prepared to depart the area, Captain Powell requested that *Zeller's* commanding officer, Commander J.E. Murphy, Jr., come alongside to take on a special cargo for the crew. When Commander Murphy had maneuvered his

Small Boy (one of several nicknames given to destroyers) alongside the giant flattop, mess deck personnel on board *Lexington* lovingly transferred, via highline, 25 gallons of ice cream to the waiting destroyermen. As a result of its generosity, *Lexington* quickly became *Zeller's* favorite carrier—an accolade not to be taken lightly when one considers that among destroyermen, carrier sailors are considered to be elitists. A standing joke among destroyer sailors, whose ships contain only the barest necessities, is that "carriers don't leave port, they take the port with them." This is in reference to the fact that carriers have many of the luxuries found in a small town—ice cream parlor, walk-in ship's stores, laundry services, library, daily newspaper, television, etc.

With the Cuban Missile Crises behind her, *Lexington* finally sailed into Pensacola Bay on December 20, 1962. After spending Christmas at anchor a few thousand yards offshore from the Pensacola Naval Air Station, *Lexington* formally relieved *Antietam* as the Navy's training carrier on

December 29, 1962.

The day before, *Antietam* skipper, Captain James H. Armstrong invited Captain Powell and members of the *Lexington* crew aboard the retiring carrier for a combination welcome/farewell ceremony. A crisp breeze blowing across the *Antietam's* flight deck that sunny December afternoon carried mixed messages. For Captain Armstrong and the crew of the *Antietam*, the whispering wind, occasionally raising to a howl, was heard as a final farewell. For Captain Powell, the crew of the *Lady Lex* and local military and civilian officials, it was the dawn of a new era for Pensacola, the "Cradle of Naval Aviation." The next morning, a cold rainy Saturday, *Antietam* cast off her lines and sailed out of the port she had called home for more than five years. Within moments of *Antietam's* departure, *Lexington's* massive hull eased alongside the Pensacola Naval Air Station's Allegheny Pier for what the Navy had previously announced would be no more than a three-year stay.

After spending the first few days of 1963 alongside the pier at the Pensacola Naval Air Station, *Lexington's* crew was eager to get on with their new mission as the training carrier for the Naval Air Training Command. The new year was barley two weeks old when *Lexington* again put to sea. But unlike previous at sea periods, when she had been dispatched in response to some world crisis, this time her primary mission was to provide a deck for student pilots to qualify as Naval aviators, and for experienced airmen to sharpen their skills so they would be ready when called upon to respond to world crises.

In July 1963, Captain Powell turned command of *Lexington* over to Captain John M. Miller. Two weeks later the carrier was back at sea conducting carrier qualifications off the coast of Key West, Florida. The following year, June 1964, *Lexington* welcomed her 14th commanding officer, Captain Quentin C. Crommelin.

During the next several years, the *Blue Ghost* became a common, reassuring sight, sailing in and out of Pensacola Bay. Her operating sched-

With only two weeks remaining of a badly needed overhaul, Lexington was hastily ordered out of dry dock for the Cuban Missile Crisis.

46

USS Zellers *served as plane guard for* Lexington
during the Cuban Missile Crisis of October 1962

ed landing, they would observe flight operations, dine with the crew on the mess decks, or with the ship's officers in the officers' wardroom, and given an opportunity to visit non-restricted work stations throughout the ship. After several hours aboard, the "*Lexington* men and women for a day" would then be assembled for a briefing on launch procedures. Then it was time for the big moment—the cat shot.

Just prior to being catapulted off the ship for the return flight back to land, each guest would be presented with a "Tailhooker" certificate, signifying that they were among the few who had landed aboard an aircraft carrier.

The *Lexington's* role as a trainer wasn't confined only to student pilots, however. Hundreds of Navy, Coast Guard and Marine Corps photographers undergoing training at the Naval Schools of Photography located at the Pensacola Naval Air Station, focused their lenses on the huge flattop. For students of the basic school (Photographer's Mate Class A School) she was the subject of photo features, magazine covers and motion picture assignments. For those military shutter-clickers in the advanced school (Photographer's Mate Class B School) *Lexington* became a target for the school's aging RC-45J twin-engine Beechcraft. As the lumbering "bug smasher," as the RC-45J was affectionately known, performed various maneuvers at varying altitudes, the student aerial cameramen honed their skills in aerial photographic techniques.

ule, despite the fact that *Lexington* generally returned to port on weekends, was undoubtedly more hectic than any fleet carrier, recording as many as 500 arrested landings per day.

By 1965, with the air war in Southeast Asia intensifying, the Navy Department decided to abandon its original plan to replace *Lexington* as the Navy's training carrier after three years. With fleet carriers of the Pacific and Atlantic Fleets rotating in and out of the South China Sea in support of the Vietnam War, it was decided that *Lexington* could best serve by continuing as a trainer. In June 1965, Captain Gordon A. Synder assumed command.

In addition to her role as a training vessel, *Lexington* assumed an additional duty during the 1960s—public relations.

When in port, particularly on weekends, hundreds of people daily boarded the *Lady Lex*. Most were local residents and tourists, but many were aviation officer cadets and newly commissioned Navy and Marine Corps officers getting their first look at an aircraft carrier, and perhaps dreaming of the day, in the not too distant future, when they would make their first solo carrier landing on board her.

Even at sea, the guests continued to visit. Military and civilian VIPs, and media personnel, were flown aboard where, after an arrest-

After turning her training duties over to Lexington, Antietam, *under the watchful eye of the NAS Pensacola-based destroyer escort* USS Tweedy *(DE-532), moves away from her Pensacola Naval Air Station berth.*

In the 1960s Lexington *set record after record for aircraft launches and recoveries.*

Those skills, aerial and ground, would later serve the sea services well, when reconnaissance and documentary photography was needed in Vietnam.

While Navy photographer trainees were recording *Lexington's* activities on film, student pilots were making history. On April 29, 1966 *Lexington* became the world's undisputed leader in arrested landings when she recorded her 150,000th "trap."

With her history-making 150,000th arrested landing neatly recorded in the ship's log, *Lexington* resumed her daily task of trapping and launching fleet and training aircraft.

Four months later, during a brief pause in operations, the crew of *Lexington*—decked out in heavily-starched white uniforms and defying the intense Florida August heat—assembled on the *Lexington's* flight deck to witness yet another change of command as Captain Snyder turned the *Lexington* helm over to Captain Jack C. Heishman.

Five months after assuming command, Captain Heishman took *Lexington* to sea as a floating laboratory for a series of tests being conducted on the Navy's newest attack plane, the A-7A Corsair II. The tests, carried out on board *Lexington* as she steamed under varying weather conditions in the Gulf of Mexico, were conducted to determine whether of not the Corsair was carrier stable. Once again, the ageless lady was doing her part in support of American operations in Southeast Asia. Less than a year later, A-7As, launched from carriers operating in the Gulf of Tonkin, were bombing targets in North Vietnam. The *Blue Ghost*, although not physically present, was still very much a part of Naval combat operations in the Pacific.

With the Corsair tests completed, *Lexington* resumed her duties as a training platform for Naval aviators. In July 1967, after more than a week of nearly round-the-clock flight operations, *Lexington* made a port call at Galveston, Texas. Since her commissioning in 1943 *Lexington* had visited hundreds of cities, overseas and at home, providing a brief period of well-deserved rest and recreation for her crew. And in light of the fact that she had made several visits to Galveston and other Gulf Coast ports since becoming the Navy's training carrier, there was no reason for the captain to believe this visit would be any different then previous ones. The crew would go ashore and Galveston residents would tour the ship.

Two days later, with the *Lexington* back at sea, en route to her home port at Pensacola, a sentry made a startling discovery. A 14-year-old Galveston girl, Lucy Ann Maldonado, had taken up temporary residence in one of *Lexington's* lifeboats. She told Captain Heishman that she wanted to visit relatives in Pensacola, so when she boarded the ship on its last day in Galveston, she had climbed into the boat, hoping she would not be discovered until the ship docked at Pensacola. After providing the teenager with a hot meal and brief medical checkup by the ship's doctor, she was promptly placed on board a helicopter and returned to Galveston. The saga of the *Lexington* stowaway was over, but on the long voyage back to Pensacola the topic of conversation centered on the young stowaway adventurer rather than the impending change of command scheduled for mid-August.

Back home in Pensacola, *Lexington* quickly

Flight deck personnel watch as a T-2 Buckeye training jet comes in for a landing during student carrier qualifications aboard the Blue Ghost.

became a beehive of activity as her sailors prepared to welcome the *Lexington's* 17th commanding officer. Captain Edward W. Gendron assumed command on August 10, 1967.

With a new skipper at the helm, *Lexington* returned to her role as a pace-setter for the fleet. On September 21, 1967, the *Blue Ghost* became the first ship in the Navy to establish a sea-going high school. Concerned that many of the enlisted men entering the Navy at that time had not graduated from high school, the *Lexington*—in cooperation with civilian educational experts from the Escambia County, Florida, school system—established a procedure whereby visiting teachers and qualified Navy personnel taught English, math, history and Naval orientation courses. After completing the required studies, High School of the High Seas (HSHS) students were awarded a General Education Development (GED) high school equivalence diploma. A number of HSHS graduates later earned commissions as Naval officers.

The following month, October 17, 1967, while en route to New Orleans, *Lexington* recorded its 200,000 arrested landing. Unfortunately the excitement of establishing yet another record may have temporary distracted Captain Gendron. After successfully navigating the ever-changing Mississippi River, *Lexington* ran into a warehouse while docking at New Orleans. A board of inquiry later absolved Captain Gendron of any possible negli-

gence in relation to the accident.

During the remainder of the decade of the sixties *Lexington* continued a routine of flight operations, interrupted only for brief yard periods. In January 1969, Captain Wayne E. Hammett assumed command and six months later, July 1, 1969, *Lexington* acquired another first, when her designation was changed from CVS to CVT (Navy Training Carrier), the first ship in Naval history to be so designated and one of only a few carriers to have had the distinction of having had four designators—CV, CVA, CVS, and CVT—with still a fifth designation—AVT—only a few short years in the future.

Although her new designation effectively removed her from further fleet service, *Lexington's* future in Naval aviation would continue for another two decades. In March 1970, Captain Cyrus Fitton assumed command.

Tours for *Lexington* skippers grew shorter during the early part of the 1970s and after only 13 months at the helm of the world's only CVT, Captain Fitton turned command of *Lexington* over to Captain Jack E. Davis in April 1972. A month later, May 22, Captain Davis and retired Captain "Benny" Wright, flying a T-2B jet trainer, recorded the ship's 300,000th arrested landing. Captain Wright had served aboard *Lexington* as an executive officer during World War II. Seven months later, Davis would relinquish command to Captain Charles C. Carter only to regain it eight months later.

In early 1973, shortly after assuming command, Captain Carter was notified by the Navy Department that *Lexington* was officially being removed from any future fleet service. With that announcement, *Lexington* was ordered to the Boston Naval Shipyard for an overhaul. In April, her repairs complete, *Lexington* prepared to leave the shipyard and promptly ran aground. Plans for a Pensacola-sponsored homecoming were put on hold while the *Lady Lex* returned to drydock to repair the damage.

Troubles continued to plague Captain Carter and in August 1973, after several incidents involving air safety aboard the carrier, he was relieved of command. Former skipper Captain Jack Davis resumed command, thus becoming the only person to command *Lexington* twice. Captain Davis remained at the helm until Captain Donald E. Moore reported aboard in November 1973.

During Captain Moore's tenure as *Lexington* CO, the proud flattop—now referred to by Gulf Coast residents as the *Blue Ghost of the Gulf Coast*—steamed more than 50,000 miles and recorded 20,000 arrested landings, including landing number 347,000. Although he was hoping to be at the helm when *Lexington* made her 350,000th "trap," fate had reserved that historic event for

Cake cutting ceremonies in honor of the 150,000 arrested landing aboard Lexington—*June 15, 1966*

Captain Thornwell F. Rush.

Within a matter of weeks after assuming command on July 9, 1975, Captain Rush was putting *Lexington* through her paces in the Gulf of Mexico, when Lt.(jg) Ted Morandi and his bombardier/navigator Lt.(jg) Dave King, approached the *Lexington*.

Within minutes, the NAS Whidbey Island, California-based Attack Squadron-128 A-6E Intruder had made a perfect carrier landing. *Lexington* had recorded her 350,000th landing.

The USS Lexington—*The* Blue Ghost—*was a major Pensacola tourist attraction for sight-seeing boats and other visitors during her in-port periods at the Pensacola Naval Air Station*

In 1972 President Richard Nixon asked drag racer Don Garlits to do a "Fly Navy Promo" with his car the Swamp Rat 16. The Lexington's Photographer's Mates were allowed to photograph the scene while assisting the photographers from "Hot Rod Magazine." They had to swear they would not sell the photographs they took to any other magazines. This is PH3 John C. Driskill's shot (left) of the Swamp Rat 16 on the flight deck, ready to race an A-7E Corsair II of VA-81 (Sunliners). Driskill made sets of the photos for Garlits and his mechanic, and Garlits signed one for Driskill (inset). All photos on this page were taken by—and are courtesy of—John C. Driskill

Clockwise from above: Swamp Rat 16, Garlits crew member, and support truck on the flight deck; Pilot of A7 Jet trying the dragster on for size; Attaching to catapult for photoshoot; "Hot Rod Magazine" photographers; Measuring out the fuel; Raising some steam on the catapult for effect

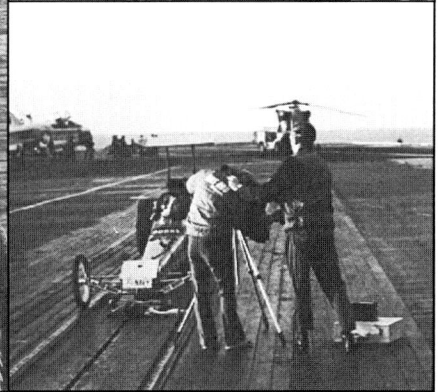

Chapter Eight

Sailors and guests stand in the island of the USS Lexington *(AVT-16) as she returns
to port following a day-long dependents' cruise.*

It seems only appropriate that the historic 350,000th arrested landing should occur during 1975, the 200th anniversary of the U.S. Navy. That was but one of many events *Lexington* used in 1975 to mark the Navy's bicentennial.

During the course of the year, *Lexington*, along with the rest of the Navy celebrated the bicentennial with parties, sports tournaments, an open house and a dependents' day cruise. No doubt, visitors to the *Blue Ghost* on October 13, 1975, did a double take when sighting what should have been the Navy Jack flying from the forward end of the flight deck. For on this date the traditional jack of 50 white stars on a blue field had been replaced by a banner bearing seven red horizontal stripes with a rattlesnake and the words "Don't Tread on Me" embossed on it. This was the First Navy Jack which was first flown on a Navy vessel in 1775. Secretary of the Navy J. William Middendorf authorized all Naval vessels to fly the First Navy Jack from October 13, 1975 until December 31, 1976.

On September 16, 1975, Air Force General Daniel (Chappie) James, a native Pensacolian and the nation's first black officer to reach four-star rank, was the guest speaker for a special ceremony at Pensacola's Washington High School. On that date in *Lexington's* history, seven of her crew members—Third Class Canuto Jocson, Petty Officer Second Class Richardo J. Kamantique, Petty Officer Third Class Samual I. Balancia, Petty Officer Third Class Augusto T. Millendez, Petty Officer Third Thomas H. Cavida, Petty Officer Third Class Zelbo Brkic and Petty Officer Third Class Migual J. Muir—became American citizens.

Lexington closed out her bicentennial celebrations November 17-18, 1975 with an all-hands party attended by more than 2,000 people at Pensacola's Seville Quarter.

As 1976 appeared on the horizon, the 1,450-man crew of *Lexington* were preparing to go Hollywood. When Universal Studios needed a World War II era carrier to recreate the Battle of Midway, the Navy agreed to permit filming aboard the *Lexington*. During the spring of 1976, *Lexington* sailors were thrilled to be sharing their work stations with the likes of such movie greats as Glenn Ford, Henry Fonda and Charlton Heston. For many *Lexington* crew members, watching the filming provided them with an understanding of what it must have been like for an earlier generation of *Lexington* sailors.

Celebrities of another type boarded *Lexington* on January 16, 1977 when boxing promoter Don King brought future world heavyweight champion Larry Holmes and a stable of fighters aboard *Lexington* for the first round of the U.S. Boxing Championships. The televised fights were seen by a worldwide audience. In May, Captain Eugene B. (Red) McDaniel, a former Vietnam prisoner of war, assumed command.

The following year, while the ship was undergoing routine repairs at a Navy shipyard, the Department of Defense announced that *Lexington*, nearing the end of her service life, would be decommissioned in 1979. Within months of the announcement however, *Lady Lex* gained a reprieve when her proposed retirement date was canceled due to the unavailability of another carrier to replace her as a training carrier. In July 1978 *Lexington* was redesignated as an Auxiliary Aircraft Landing Training Ship (AVT). Three months later, Captain Philip E. Johnson relieved Captain McDaniel as *Lexington's* skipper.

In October 1979, *Lexington* (AVT-16) departed Pensacola for an overhaul at the Philadelphia Naval Shipyard. The $32 million overhaul would keep *Lexington* in commission until 1984. In May 1980, after eight

Workmen at the Philadelphia Navy Shipyard discuss what needs to be done prior to moving Lexington *into drydock.*

In 1980 Lexington *was thrust into the spotlight, when she became the first ship in U.S. Naval history to count women among its crew.*

entered its last years of service, women made up nearly 25 percent of the total ship's complement of 1,448 sailors.

1981 brought good news to the crew of the *Lexington* and Pensacola residents, when the Navy announced on May 10th that *Lexington* would not be taken out of service until at least 1989.

The entire Florida Panhandle was beaming with excitement in September 1981 when Pensacola High School graduate, Lt.(jg) Pat Denkler became the first woman to land an aircraft on board *Lexington*. Women had not only been added to the *Lexington* crew, they had entered and conquered the previously all-male world of Naval aviation.

In December 1981, the *Lexington* helm shifted to Captain James W. Ryan.

A few months later, in April 1982 while conducting carrier qualification landings off Key West, Florida, *Lexington* and her plane guard helicopters from Pensacola's only fleet ready aircraft squadron, HC-16, discovered three people adrift in the Gulf of Mexico. As pilots Lt.(jg) David J. Pech and Ens. Shane Eyer positioned their helicopter over the water-logged men, Petty Officer Second Class Daniel Becker and Airman Gregory Lambert hoisted them aboard the helicopter. Safely aboard the *Lady Lex*, it was learned they were Cuban fishermen whose boat had capsized a day earlier. The fishermen were later turned over to U.S. Immigration officials for return to Cuba.

In mid-1982, *Lexington* entered a Jacksonville, Florida shipyard for a routine yearly maintenance period. Returning to Pensacola in early November, the *Blue Ghost* quickly resumed her duties of providing a landing platform for fledgling Naval aviators. By early 1983, with an average of 2,000 aircraft per year landing aboard the *Lexington*, it had become obvious that if the *Lady Lex* was to continue at the same pace, a major overhaul was called for. Conservative estimates indicated that it would cost in excess of a $100 million to keep the 40-year-old carrier operating until her planned 1989 decommissioning date.

In June 1983, Captain Harold J. Bernsen became *Lexington's* 29th commanding officer. In July, Captain Bernsen addressed the Pensacola Press Club and extended an invitation to members of the local media to visit the ship. On August 19, 1983 some 30 media rep-

months of repairs, *Lexington* returned to the Cradle of Naval Aviation, where thousands of area residents eagerly awaited her return. In June, Captain William H. Green Jr., reported aboard as *Lexington's* 27th commanding officer.

Three months later on August 18, 1980, *Lexington* was again thrust into the spotlight, when she became the first ship in U.S. Naval history to welcome women aboard as crew members. Although the role of women in the Navy began to change during the 1980s, *Lexington* remained the only aircraft carrier in the U.S. Navy to routinely count women among its crew. As the ship resentatives, some of whom felt the Navy could best be served by replacing *Lexington* with a newer ship as the Navy's training carrier, boarded *Lexington* for lunch with Captain Bernsen and a tour of the ship. The stories which appeared in the local press during the following weeks praised the *Lexington*, recounted her proud history, and made pleas for the funding necessary to keep the grand dame of the Gulf Coast afloat. The captain had taken full advantage of the power of the press. In October *Lexington* entered a shipyard at Mobile, Alabama for a three-month upkeep period.

Following her yard period at Mobile's Bender Shipyard, *Lexington* renewed her hectic pace of carrier qualifications. Only this time, those long hours at sea were more entertaining for the crew. In January 1984 *Lexington* established a radio station—WLEX—which went on the air daily during at-sea periods, from 6 a.m. until midnight, with news, weather, sports and the top 40 rock and country tunes. A similar service, which also included the showing of the latest movies, was provided over the carrier's closed-circuit television station, WLEX-TV.

Lexington rests alongside the mothballed battleship USS Wisconsin *(BB-64) and other decommissioned ships during her 1985 overhaul at the Philadelphia Naval Shipyard.*

Although the ship's mission was still the same—serving as a training carrier—at least the crew now had something to help fill the sometimes long periods between launches and recoveries.

WLEX-radio and WLEX-TV were utilized to their maximum on March 8, 1984, when *Lexington* made its 250,000th steam catapult shot.

In late 1984, after months of speculation and on-again, off-again appropriations, *Lexington* was finally given the green light for an $83.3 million overhaul. An earlier appropriation of $127 million slated for overhauling the 40-year-old carrier was withdrawn by the Senate Subcommittee on Defense Appropriations. Without a major overhaul *Lexington* would not be able to continue in operation until her previously announced 1989 decommissioning date.

As the dark clouds of doom were gathering on the horizon, Navy and local elected officials, assisted by the local news media, made an urgent appeal to the Senate Subcommittee on Defense Appropriations to restore funding for the necessary repairs.

Although the Subcommittee refused to restore the full $127 million, they did agree to allocate $83.3 million, which Navy officials believed would keep the grand old flattop operating until the end of the decade.

With the battle of the budget at least partially won, Captain Bernsen surrendered command of the *Lady Lex* to Captain Paul M. Feran in December 1984.

When *Lexington* returned to NAS Pensacola in mid-August 1985, after a nine-and-a-half month overhaul at the Philadelphia Naval Shipyard, her crew was filled with mixed emotions. Most of her critical machinery had been overhauled and her wooden flight deck, long a source of problems, had

Shipyard workers and friends bid the Lexington *goodbye as the overhauled carrier sets sail for Pensacola.*

Thousands of Pensacola area residents, family members and officials were on hand at NAS Pensacola to greet the Lady Lex when she returned to the Cradle of Naval Aviation after an extended yard period.

been replaced by steel.

The desperately need overhaul pretty much assured that *Lexington* would remain in commission until 1990. Although her future appeared somewhat brighter, her days in the Cradle of Naval Aviation appeared to be numbered. On July 2, 1985, the Navy announced that under the Navy's proposed strategic homeporting plan, *Lexington* would be replaced in Pensacola by the fleet battle carrier *USS Kitty Hawk* (CV-63). The Navy's only training carrier would then be reassigned to Corpus Christi, Texas, where she would continue her role as a training carrier. The strategic homeporting plan was part of Secretary of the Navy John Lehman's proposal for a 600-ship Navy.

In 1986, *Lexington* joined with her sister carriers Navy-wide, to celebrate the 75th Anniversary of Naval aviation. *Lexington*, however, as she had managed to do for more then 40 years, upstaged her sisters when master showman Bob Hope saluted Naval aviation with a nationally televised program from her flight deck.

In November Captain Feran relinquished command to Captain Haywood G. Sprouse.

Hollywood returned to the *Blue Ghost* in 1987 with the filming of the ABC-TV mini-series "War and Remembrance." The $140 million mini-series starring Robert Mitchum briefly returned the famed carrier, through the magic of television, to World War II. During the course of filming, *Lexington* played the role of two of her war-time sisters, *USS Enterprise* and *USS Yorktown*, plus the role of the Japanese carrier *Akagi*.

Naval Aviation 75th Anniversary May 1986

On May 7, 1986 Naval aviation celebrated its 75th anniversary. Because the *USS Lexington*—the *Blue Ghost*—was based in the Cradle of Naval Aviation it was only fitting that the *Lexington* was selected as the platform from which a nationwide television anniversary special would be telecast. The May 7-8th taping for Bob Hope's annual "Bob Hope Special" to be broadcast over the NBC television network, included some of the biggest names in show business such as movie stars Elizabeth Taylor, Phylicia Rashad, Brooke Shields, Sammy Davis Jr., Don Johnson, Jonathan Winters and country music stars, Barbara Mandrell and Mac Davis.

During the two days of actual taping and several of preparation, *Lexington* men and women played host not only to Hollywood elite and government officials, but to the entire world.

Because of the anniversary special, many Americans saw the famous carrier for the first time, and for others around the nation the pictures of *Lexington* brought back vivid memories of another era. For them, the *Blue Ghost* had returned to life.

In October, *Lexington* joined in a partnership with A.A. Dixon Elementary School in Pensacola's inner city. The alliance between ship and school assured students with poor academic records that help was available from selected crew members of the *Lady Lex*. During the signing of the agreement between the school and *Lexington*, Captain Sprouse recalled that 20 years earlier, the Escambia County School District and *Lexington* had joined forces to insure that *Lexington* sailors who had not graduated from high school were given a second chance to receive their high school diploma. The alliance between *Lexington* and A.A. Dixon completed the educational circle which had been established between the Escambia County School District and the *Lady Lex* in 1967.

In May 1988, one the *Lexington's* most popular commanding officers, Captain C. Flack Logan reported aboard.

Shortly after Logan assumed command, *Lexington* returned to the yards for $10 million worth of renovations. In addition to routine maintenance, the ship received major repairs on two of her four high pressure turbines. While

A pilot's view of the Lady Lex *(above), as the* Lexington's *C-1A cargo plane (above) prepares for its final trap.*

shipyard workers and the *Lexington* crew were struggling to keep the 45-year-old carrier steaming, some of the aircraft which had been landing on her flight deck for years, were being phased out. Within a month of completing her 1988 yard upkeep period, the *Lexington's* C-1A Trader cargo/passenger plane made its last landing aboard the *Blue Ghost*.

During the course of *Lexington's* yard period, negotiations had been quietly taking place between the City of Pensacola and the Navy. In order for the Pensacola Naval Air Station to prepare for the projected 1990 arrival of *Kitty Hawk*, the air station's Allegheny Pier would have to be vacated. If arrangements couldn't be made to berth *Lexington* at the city's municipal pier, the Navy would be forced to transfer *Lexington* to Corpus Christi nearly two years early. Two years without a carrier based in the City of Five Flags would create an economic hardship on the people of Pensacola and Escambia County.

On July 15, 1988 the Pensacola City Council approved an agreement to let the *Lady Lex* dock at the Port of Pensacola.

During the remainder of 1988, while *Lexington* was conducting carrier qualifications for student and fleet pilots in the Gulf of Mexico, dredging equipment was at work deepening the channel leading to Pensacola's Bayfront Auditorium.

With the channel growing deeper by the day, Navy and city officials were making plans for *Lexington's* arrival at the Port of Pensacola. As the hot humid temperatures of summer gave way to autumn *Lexington* prepared for what would be her last Christmas at the Pensacola Naval Air Station. As 1989 dawned on the horizon, Mayor Vince Whibbs and the Pensacola City Council stepped up their plans for a gala 1940s-style celebration to commemorate the arrival of the *Lady Lex* at the Port of Pensacola.

After making its final landing aboard the Lexington *in 1988, the Grumman C1A Trader, folded its wings and retired from active service.*

Chapter Nine

As the Lexington *slipped out of her berth at the Pensacola Naval Air Station for the Port of Pensacola, Navy Patrol boats were called out to keep sight-seeing boats at a safe distance.*

On April 26, 1989, with a blast of the ship's whistle, *Lexington* shifted colors and eased away from the pier she had called home for nearly 27 years. An hour and twenty-seven minutes later, at precisely 4:47 p.m., the *Blue Ghost* shifted colors again as the first line went over at her new berth at the Port of Pensacola.

With dozens of late 1930s and early 1940s vintage automobiles parked along South Palafox Street in downtown Pensacola, thousands of area residents, many of them decked out in 1940s fashions, crowded onto the pier and parking lots of Pensacola's Bayfront Auditorium to welcome the *Blue Ghost* home from a make believe wartime cruise. The welcoming ceremony, which some longtime residents claimed was the largest such celebration since World War II, continued throughout the weekend of April 29-30th. The move to downtown Pensacola was at the time viewed as the closing of a chapter in the history of Naval aviation. In accordance with the Navy's strategic homeporting plans, the next carrier slated to call the Cradle of Naval Aviation home was supposed to have been the *USS Kitty Hawk*, the lead ship of a Gulf of Mexico-based carrier battle group.

After six months of uneventful operations out of the Port of Pensacola, tragedy raised its ugly head in October 1989 claiming the lives of five people aboard *Lexington* and injuring 19 others. On the night of October 29, a T-2 Buckeye training jet from Training Squadron-19 based at NAS Meridian, Mississippi was attempting to land aboard the *Lex* when it crashed into the ship's island, killing the student pilot, Ensign Steven E. Pontell, three *Lexington* flight deck personnel—Petty Officer Third Class Burnett Kilgore, Jr., ABH3 Timmy L. Garoutte, and Airman Lisa L. Mayo—and civilian contract employee Byron G. Courvelle. Tragically, Airman Mayo had the dubious distinction of establishing another *Lexington* first—the first female sailor to be killed aboard an American aircraft carrier in the line of duty.

In an emotional pierside press conference on October 30, Captain Logan said the T-2 was coming in "low and slow." Fighting to keep the emotion from his voice, Logan told reporters that the landing signal officer had attempted to wave the plane off, but its nose pitched up and the T-2 inverted and smashed into the island just below the ship's control tower.

That accident, combined with several others throughout the Navy during 1989, prompted the Chief of Naval Operations, Admiral Carlisle A.H. Throst, to order an unprecedented Navy-wide, two-day safety stand-down in November 1989.

If the threat of communism was responsible for the re-birth of the *USS Lexington* in 1955, then it could also be argued that the demise of the communist threat in the late 1980s was at least partially responsible for the acceleration of *Lexington's* decommissioning. In September 1990, after months of rumor and speculation, the Navy formally announced that *Lexington* would be decommissioned in Pensacola in 1991. The announcement further stated that the *USS Forestall* (CV-59) would replace *Lexington*.

Forestall, unlike *Lexington's* previously announced replacement in Pensacola, the *USS Kitty Hawk*, was to be converted to an AVT and serve in the same capacity as *Lexington* had—as a training carrier—homeported at Pensacola. Changes in the world political climate and worsening economic woes at home combined to change the make up of the U.S. Navy. Plans for a 600-ship fleet, including 14 carrier battle groups, were scrapped and the fate of Gulf Coast strategic homeporting remained in doubt. It was certain, however, that after nearly half a century of service, the *Blue Ghost* was ready for retirement.

With the announcement of *Lexington's* pending retirement, a feasibility study was launched to determine if it would be economical for the city to try and acquire *Lexington* as a floating museum. The project was later continued by the *Lexington* Museum Foundation, a private group formed to raise funds and support to keep the historic carrier in the City of Five Flags.

After months of debate and political maneuvering, the Pensacola City Council in a 7-3 vote, decided on August 29, 1991 to reject the *Lexington* Foundation's bid to keep the historic carrier in Pensacola as a memorial and museum. Three other cities—Mobile, Alabama; Corpus Christi, Texas; and Quincy, Massachusetts—made formal application with the Navy to obtain *Lexington* as a museum ship.

On December 18, 1990, *Lexington's* 33rd and final skipper, Captain William H. Kennedy reported aboard.

With a new skipper at the helm, the *Lady Lex* in January 1991 resumed her task of training Naval aviators. But twice during the first two months of 1991, the ship's operating schedule had to be modified because of mounting mechanical difficulties. Still, the grand dame of aircraft carriers struggled to carry out her duties. On March 8, 1991, Lt. Kathy Owens, a 27-year-old native of Cincinnati, Ohio made landing 493,760 on board the *Blue Ghost*.

What should have been a routine landing for the VCR-40 pilot and crew of the C-2 cargo jet—copilot Lt. Paul Villagomez and crewmembers AMH1 Donnie Kicklighter and AD2 Mark Pemrick—was entered in the history books as the last arrested landing aboard the *USS Lexington*. Less than two weeks later, Navy officials, citing engineering

and safety problems, suspended all further operations. The long career of the *USS Lexington*, the ship that couldn't be sunk, had come to an end.

Time had accomplished what the entire Japanese fleet couldn't—end the life of the *Blue Ghost*.

On May 2, 1991, the *Lady Lex*, unable to operate under her own power, was unceremoniously towed from the Port of Pensacola back to the Pensacola Naval Air Station where she was decommissioned on November 8, 1991.

Over the next several months her crew removed stores and other usable items from the ship and sealed her stack and catapults. As summer gave way to autumn the crew of the proud carrier steadily dwindled away until only a couple hundred sailors remained for the actual decommissioning ceremony.

On November 8, 1991, more than 4,000 spectators, including several dozen members of *Lex-*

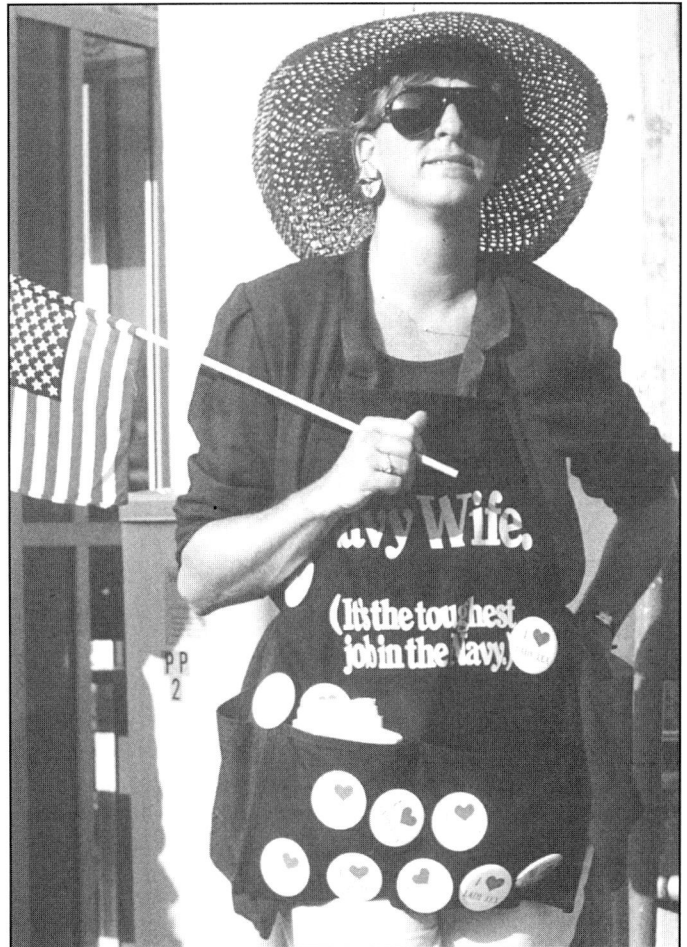

While the Lexington *was underway for the one- hour "cruise," thousands of Pensacolians, including the* Lexington *executive officer's wife, Jamia Eckart (above) were assembling on the Pensacola waterfront to welcome the* Lexington *to downtown Pensacola.*

Investigators (above, right) examine the wreckage of a T-2 Buckeye training jet which crashed aboard Lexington *during carrier qualifications on the night of October 26, 1989. The crash killed five people, including the pilot, and injured 19 others*

Allison Welden (below), a sailor stationed aboard the auxiliary aircraft landing training ship USS LEXINGTON, *is helped along the pier by her brother Richard and a friend following the ship's return to its home port. The injury to Welden's leg was not sustained in the accident*

Family members and friends of Lexington crew members (left) wait for the Lexington to return to port after the fatal crash.

Line handlers (below) stand by to secure the Blue Ghost after returning to port following the fatal crash of the T-2C Buckeye.

ington's World War II crew, and news media representatives from around the nation, gathered at the air station's Allegheny Pier which had been home to the *Lexington* for nearly 30 years to bid the grand old warship a final farewell.

Although it was her time, *Lexington* seemed to fight to the last minute. The day of her decommissioning ceremony was one of the coldest November days ever recorded on the Florida Panhandle. It was as though *Lexington* was attempting to defy the odds and live to fight another day.

With her crew gone and machinery shut down, *Lexington*, now little more than a gray steel hulk, remained in Pensacola until January 1992 when she was once again taken in tow for a five-day voyage to her final destination.

In an emotional pier side press conference a day after a T-2C Buckeye aircraft crashed into the carrier's tower during a touch-and-go-practice landing on October 29, 1989, Captain Flack Logan, Commanding Officer of the aircraft carrier USS LEXINGTON *(AVT 16), attempted to explain to reporters what caused the crash, which killed the student pilot and four others*

As the Lady Lex *left the Cradle of Naval Aviation for the last time, well-wishers gathered along the seawall to bid her bon voyage (above).*

USS Lexington *Museum of the Bay, Corpus Christi, Texas (below)*

Chapter Ten
The Commanding Officers of the USS Lexington

Capt. Felix B. Stump
February 1943 — April 1944

Capt. Ernest W. Litch
April 1944 — January 1945

Capt. Thomas H. Robbins
January 1945 — November 1945

Capt. Bradford E. Crow
November 1945 — October 1946

Capt. Alexander S. Heyward, Jr.
August 1955 — October 1956

Capt. John W. Cannon
October 1956 — September 1957

Capt. Burl L. Bailey
September 1957 — July 1958

Capt. James R. Reedy
July 1958 — June 1959

Capt. Stanley E. Ruehlow
June 1959 — July 1960

Capt. Stockton B. Strong
July 1960 — July 1961

Capt. Hart D. Hilton
July 1961 — July 1962

Capt. Lucien C. Powell
July 1962 — October 1962

Capt. John M. Miller
July 1963 — June 1964

Capt. Quentin C. Crommelin
June 1964 — June 1965

Capt. Gordon A. Snyder
June 1965 — August 1966

Capt. Jack C. Heishmann
August 1966 — August 1967

Capt. Edward W. Gendron
August 1967 — January 1969

Capt. Wayne E. Hammett
January 1969 — March 1970

Capt. Cyrus F. Fitton
March 1970 — April 1971

Capt. Jack. E. Davis
April 1971 — December 1972

Capt. Charles C. Carter
December 1972 — August 1973

Capt. Donald E. Moore
November 1973 — July 1975

Capt. Thornwell F. Rush
July 1975 — May 1977

Capt. Eugene B. McDaniel
May 1977 — November 1978

Capt. Philip E. Johnson
November 1978 — June 1980

Capt. William H. Green, Jr.
June 1980 — December 1981

Capt. James W. Ryan
December 1981 —June 1983

Capt. Harold J. Bernsen
June 1983 — December 1984

71

Capt. Paul M. Feran
December 1984 — November 1986

Capt. Haywood G. Sprouse
November 1986 — May 1988

Capt. C. Flack Logan
May 1988 — December 1990

Capt. William H. Kennedy
December 1990 — November 1991

USS LEXINGTON
MUSEUM ON THE BAY
★ ★ ★
CORPUS CHRISTI, TEXAS